Living and Working in English

Joan Saslow

Regional Consultant Board

Ann Belletire *Illinois*	**Sandra Bergman** *New York*	**Sherie Burnette** *Texas*	**Michael Feher** *Massachusetts*	**Susan B. Kanter** *Texas*
Brigitte Marshall *California*	**Monica Oliva** *Florida*	**Mary E. O'Neill** *Virginia*	**Grace Tanaka** *California*	**Marcia L. Taylor** *Indiana*

Edwina Hoffman
Series Advisor

LONGMAN ON THE WEB

Longman.com offers online resources for teachers and students. Access our Companion Websites, our online catalog, and our local offices around the world.

Longman English Success offers online courses to give learners flexible study options. Courses cover General English, Business English, and Exam Preparation.

Visit us at longman.com and englishsuccess.com.

Workplace Plus: Living and Working in English 3

Pearson Education, 10 Bank Street, White Plains, NY 10606

Vice president, director of publishing: Allen Ascher
Senior acquisitions editor: Marian Wassner
Senior development editor: Marcia Schonzeit
Vice president, director of design and production: Rhea Banker
Executive managing editor: Linda Moser
Senior production editor: Christine Lauricella
Production supervisor: Liza Pleva
Senior manufacturing manager: Patrice Fraccio
Manufacturing supervisor: Dave Dickey
Cover design: Ann France
Text design: Ann France
Text composition and art direction: Word and Image Design Studio Inc.
Illustrations: Craig Attebery, pp. 1, 3, 6, 7, 19, 20, 34, 44, 48, 58, 60, 61, 62, 74, 86, 87, 88, 89, 90, 105, 118, 119; Brian Hughes, pp. 16, 17, 18, 25, 29, 30, 31, 39, 43, 46, 47, 72, 73, 83, 99, 100, 101, 115; Dave McKay, pp. 57, 67, 102, 109, 127, 128, 137; Suzanne Mogensen, pp. 21, 37, 39, 53, 66, 75, 85, 87, 95, 111; NSV Productions, pp. 4, 15, 16, 28, 33, 44, 45, 71, 75, 77, 78, 79, 80, 81, 84, 102, 103, 113, 114, 117, 122, 123; Dusan Petricic, pp. 2, 31, 32, 108; Meryl Treatner, pp. 5, 8, 22, 23, 36, 50, 64, 76, 92, 106, 120, 134; Anna Veltfort, pp. 5, 12, 26, 40, 54, 68, 82, 89, 96, 105, 124, 129, 138; Word & Image Design, pp. 11, 14, 17, 32, 35, 39, 42, 53, 59, 62, 70, 95, 98, 108, 110, 116, 123, 126, 128, 133, 137, 139, 152, 153, 154, 155, 156, 157, 158, 160, 161, 162, 163
p. 159: Reprinted by permission of New York City Department of Sanitation, Bureau of Waste Prevention, Reuse and Recycling.
Photography: Gilbert Duclos, pp. 2, 3, 4, 5, 9, 10, 16, 17, 18, 19, 23, 30, 31, 32, 33, 35, 37, 39, 43, 44, 45, 46, 47, 48, 49, 51, 58, 59, 60, 61, 65, 72, 75, 77, 86, 87, 88, 89, 93, 95, 100, 101, 102, 103, 107, 114, 115, 116, 117, 121, 128, 129, 130, 131, 133, 135

Library of Congress Cataloging-in-Publication Data

Saslow, Joan M.
  Workplace plus, living and working in English. Student book 3 / Joan Saslow.
  p. cm.
  ISBN 0-13-094329-0
  1. English language—Textbooks for foreign speakers. 2. Life skills—Problems, exercises, etc. 3. Work—Problems, exercises, etc. I. Title: Workplace plus. II. Title.

3 4 5 6 7 8 9 10—WC—07 06 05 04 03

Contents

Scope and sequence

Unit	Workplace Skills	Life Skills	Civics Concepts	Social Language	Grammar
1 **Your life and work** page 1	• Prepares for job interview • Completes application • Requests letter of recommendation • Describes skills and abilities	• Engages in small talk • Gets to know someone • Asks for references	• Appropriate job interview dress and demeanor	How to • initiate conversations • give and accept compliments • get to know someone	• The present perfect continuous • Gerunds for describing likes, dislikes, and skills
2 **Your environment** page 15	• Requests and gives directions inside a building • Offers and gives assistance • Gives directions to a place	• Demonstrates elevator etiquette • Gives directions for transportation • Uses maps and building directories	• Appropriate punctuality for social invitations	How to • extend and accept invitations • ask for directions • tell and ask others for directions • make plans to meet	• Imperatives for directions, warnings, requests, and suggestions • Indirect commands
3 **Your equipment and machines** page 29	• Tells employer about equipment breakdown • Troubleshoots a problem	• Discusses a product warranty • Completes a proof-of-purchase card • Uses telephone product service lines	• Rights afforded by product warranties • Employer expectations that workers report equipment breakdowns	How to • admit a possible error • reassure a worried person • empathize • express worry about consequences	• The passive voice • Review: Irregular past participles
4 **Your customers** page 43	• Explains a discontinued item • Discusses a safety recall • Offers to make good • Improves a quality-control problem • Offers service	• Requests a brand • Asks for service in a gas station • Acts on a product recall • Explains conditions • Writes consumer complaint letters	• Consumer Product Safety Commission and product safety recalls • Civic responsibility for the environment • EPA rules	How to • confirm another's opinion • express disappointment • express regret • offer an alternative	• *Used to* • Comparisons with *as* and *not as* • Review: Comparative forms
5 **Your time** page 57	• Understands consequences of lateness • Clarifies job expectations • Discusses payment, hours, and overtime pay	• Discusses payment • Computes pay • Understands importance of punctuality • Reschedules events	• Fair Labor Standards Act: minimum wage and entitlement to overtime pay • Company time vs. personal time	How to • reschedule events • provide reasons • interrupt politely • ask for repetition • ask for permission • clarify expectations	• Verbs followed by infinitives • Verbs followed by objects and infinitives

SCANS Competencies	SCANS Foundation Skills					
	Listening	**Speaking**	**Reading**	**Writing**	**Thinking**	**Personal Qualities**
• Interpersonal: Interprets and communicates • Information: Organizes data	Understands • small talk • interview questions	• Role-plays a job interview • Relates a personal experience	Reads • application forms • advice about interview etiquette	• Completes employment applications • Charts job skills • Writes a composition	• Classifies behavior as appropriate and inappropriate	• Demonstrates courtesy and sociability • Demonstrates self-management
• Information: Acquires and evaluates data related to locations • Interpersonal: Negotiates and plans with culturally diverse companions	Understands • requests for assistance • invitations • work-related directions	• Instructs co-workers • Relates a personal experience	Reads • maps, plans, and diagrams • advice about social behavior • handwritten directions	• Writes directions • Charts activities and locations • Writes an informal note • Writes a composition	• Interprets maps • Analyzes problems depicted in picture • Compares and contrasts map resources	• Demonstrates individual responsibility by assisting others • Demonstrates sociability
• Information: Acquires and evaluates data • Technology: Maintains equipment and troubleshoots problems	Understands • concerns over errors • equipment problems	• Describes equipment breakdowns • Uses telephone service lines • Relates a personal experience	Reads • warranties • advice about reporting breakdowns • a repair or replace order • service receipts	• Fills in a proof-of-purchase card • Charts machinery breakdowns • Writes a composition	• Interprets a product warranty • Compares and contrasts service receipts	• Demonstrates individual responsibility by reporting equipment breakdowns • Demonstrates integrity
• Interpersonal: Serves customers • Information: Acquires and evaluates data	Understands • product recall announcements • attributes of brands and products	• Role-plays a product recall • Offers to make good • Relates a personal experience	Reads • CPSC safety recalls • letters of complaint • advice about environmental hazards	• Writes a complaint letter and response • Charts defective products • Writes a composition	• Compares and contrasts consumer behavior in a native country with the U.S.A. • Compares and contrasts present and past life	• Demonstrates individual responsibility as it relates to the environment and product safety
• Resources: Knows how to allocate time • Information: Interprets and communicates information • Systems: Understands organizational systems	Understands • discussions of wages and hours • jobs and duties • employer's instructions	• Discusses payment and hours, hours, overtime pay • Advises co-workers • Relates a personal experience	Reads • employment policies and procedures • about minimum wage • job postings • advice about punctuality at work	• Charts occupations of classmates • Completes paragraphs • Writes a composition	• Compares and contrasts payment options • Understands consequences	• Demonstrates individual responsibility as it relates to punctuality • Demonstrates self-management • Demonstrates sociability

SCANS Competencies	SCANS Foundation Skills					
	Listening	Speaking	Reading	Writing	Thinking	Personal Qualities
• <u>Interpersonal</u>: Teaches others; Teams with partner • <u>Information</u>: Acquires and evaluates data; Uses computer to process information	Understands • conversations about bargains • information on unit pricing • conversations about ordering supplies	• Explains purchasing decisions • Orders over the phone • Relates a personal experience	Reads • unit pricing information and labels • about ordering online or by mail	• Charts information on units of measure • Completes a mail order • Writes a composition	• Compares and contrasts values • Draws conclusions • Classifies products by unit of measure	• Demonstrates self-management
• <u>Interpersonal</u>: Works on teams and teaches others • <u>Information</u>: Interprets and communicates information	Understands • conversations about disputes between neighbors	• Inquires about rules and laws • Advises others • Relates a personal experience	Reads • advice about community rules and laws • summons for violation of a rule	• Charts signs related to laws • Writes a composition	• Compares and contrasts customs and laws in a native country and U.S.A.	• Demonstrates sociability through consideration of others • Demonstrates individual responsibility for knowing the law
• <u>Interpersonal</u>: Negotiates and works in teams • <u>Systems</u>: Monitors and corrects performance • <u>Information</u>: Acquires and evaluates data	Understands • public service announce-ments about safe food-handling information	• Reports a food problem • Advises others on food safety • Relates a personal experience	Reads • medicine labels • about food safety • about over-the-counter medications	• Charts remedies for aliments • Writes a composition	• Analyzes medications • Compares food-handling customs • Applies warnings on medications	• Demonstrates sociability • Demonstrates integrity by representing employer honestly
• <u>Interpersonal</u>: Works in teams • <u>Information</u>: Acquires and evaluates data • <u>Systems</u>: Understands organizational systems	Understands • descriptions of banking services • conversations about credit	• Discusses debt • Inquires about credit counseling services • Relates a personal experience	Reads • credit card bills • about credit counseling services in the Yellow Pages • consumer information from the FTC Web site	• Charts bank services and accounts • Writes checks • Writes a composition	• Compares bank services • Solves debt-related problems • Decides how much to pay on a credit card bill	• Demonstrates individual responsibility to live within one's means • Demonstrates self-manage-ment of personal finances
• <u>Information</u>: Interprets and communicates information • <u>Systems</u>: Monitors and corrects performance	Understands • radio advice programs on interviewing "tips"	• Responds to an ad • Role-plays a job interview • Discusses career goals • Relates a personal experience	Reads • classified ads • advice about employee-boss communica-tion	• Writes a cover letter to apply for a job • Completes a performance review form • Writes a composition	• Identifies reasons to change jobs	• Demonstrates sociability • Demonstrates individual responsibility by giving reasons for actions

Acknowledgments

The author wishes to acknowledge with gratitude the following consultants and reviewers—our partners in the development of *Workplace Plus*.

Regional Consultant Board

The following people have participated on an ongoing basis in shaping the content and approach of *Workplace Plus*:

Ann Belletire, Northern Illinois University–Business and Industry Services, Oak Brook, Illinois • **Sandra Bergman**, Instructional Facilitator, Alternative, Adult, and Continuing Education Program, New York City Board of Education • **Sherie Burnette**, Assistant Dean, Workforce Education, Brookhaven College of the Dallas County Community College District, Farmers Branch, Texas • **Michael Feher**, Boston Chinatown Neighborhood Center, Boston, Massachusetts • **Susan B. Kanter**, Instructional Supervisor, Continuing Education and Contract Training, Houston Community College-Southwest, Houston, Texas • **Brigitte Marshall**, Consultant, Albany, California • **Monica Oliva**, Educational Specialist, Miami-Dade County Public Schools, Miami, Florida • **Mary E. O'Neill**, Coordinator of Community Education, ESL, Northern Virginia Community College—Annandale Campus, Annandale, Virginia • **Grace Tanaka**, Professor of ESL, Santa Ana College School of Continuing Education; ESL Facilitator, Centennial Education Center, Santa Ana, California • **Marcia L. Taylor**, Workplace Instructor, Joblink, Ispat-Inland Inc., East Chicago, Indiana

Reviewers

The following people shared their perspectives and made suggestions either by reviewing manuscript or participating in editorial conferences with the author and editors:

Leslie Jo Adams, Santa Ana College–Centennial Education Center, Santa Ana, California • **Sandra Anderson**, El Monte-Rosemead Adult School, El Monte, California • **Marcy Berquist**, San Diego Community College District, San Diego, California • **Robert Breitbard**, District School Board of Collier County, Naples, Florida • **Ruth Brigham**, A.C.C.E.S.S., Boston, Massachusetts • **Donna Burns**, Mt. San Antonio College, Walnut, California • **Eric Burton**, Downington Area School District, Downington, Pennsylvania • **Michael James Climo**, West Los Angeles College, Culver City, California • **Teresa Costa**, The English Center, Miami, Florida • **Robert Cote**, Miami-Dade County Public Schools, Miami, Florida • **Georgette Davis**, North Orange County Community College District, Orange County, California • **Janet Ennis**, Santa Ana College–Centennial Education Center, Santa Ana, California • **Peggy Fergus**, Northern Illinois University–Business and Industry Services, Oak Brook, Illinois • **Oliva Fernandez**, Hillsborough County Public Schools–Adult & Community Education, Tampa, Florida • **Elizabeth Fitzgerald**, Hialeah Adult & Community Center, Hialeah, Florida • **Marty Furch**, Palomar College, San Diego, California • **Eric Glicker**, North Orange County Community College District, Orange County, California • **Steve Gwynne**, San Diego Community College District, San Diego, California • **Victoria Hathaway**, DePaul University, Chicago, Illinois • **Jeffrey L. Janulis**, Richard J. Daley College, City Colleges of Chicago, Chicago, Illinois • **Mary Karamourtopoulos**, Northern Essex Community College, Haverhill, Massachusetts • **Shirley Kelly**, Brookhaven College of the Dallas County Community College District, Farmers Branch, Texas • **Marilou Kessler**, Jewish Vocational Service–Vocational English Program, Chicago, Illinois • **Henry Kim**, North Orange County Community College District, Orange County, California • **Dr. Maria H. Koonce**, Broward County Public Schools, Ft. Lauderdale, Florida • **John Kostovich**, South Texas Community College–Intensive English Program, McAllen, Texas • **Jacques LaCour**, Mt. Diablo Adult Education, Concord, California • **Beatrice Liebman**, Miami Sunset Adult Center, Miami, Florida • **Doris Lorden**, Wright College–Workforce Training Center, Chicago, Illinois • **Mike Lowman**, Coral Gables Adult Education Center, Coral Gables, Florida • **Lois Maharg**, Delaware Technical and Community College • **Vicki Moore**, El Monte-Rosemead Adult School, El Monte, California • **Deborah Nash**, School Board of Palm Beach County Schools, West Palm Beach, Florida • **Cindy Neubrech**, Mt. San Antonio College, Walnut, California • **Patricia Peabody**, Broward County Public Schools, Ft. Lauderdale, Florida • **Joe A. Perez**, Hillsborough County Public Schools, Tampa, Florida • **Diane Pinkley**, Teacher's College, Columbia University, New York, New York • **Kay Powell**, Santa Ana College–Centennial Education Center, Santa Ana, California • **Wendy Rader**, San Diego Community College District, San Diego, California • **Don Robison**, Jewish Vocational Service–Workplace Literacy, Chicago, Illinois • **Richard Sasso**, Triton College, River Grove, Illinois • **Mary Segovia**, El Monte-Rosemead Adult School, El Monte, California • **Laurie Shapero**, Miami-Dade Community College, Miami, Florida • **Sara Shapiro**, El Monte-Rosemead Adult School, El Monte, California • **Samanthia Spence**, Richland College, Dallas, Texas • **JoAnn Stehy**, North Orange County Community College District, Orange County, California • **Margaret Teske**, Mt. San Antonio College, Walnut, California • **Dung Tran**, North Orange County Community College District, Orange County, California • **Claire Valier**, School District of Palm Beach County, West Palm Beach, Florida • **Catherine M. Waterman**, Rancho Santiago Community College, Santa Ana, California • **James Wilson**, Mt. San Antonio College, Walnut, California

To the teacher

Workplace Plus: Living and Working in English is a four-level course in English as a second language which starts at the absolute beginner language level.* The course prepares adults for self-sufficiency in the three principal areas of their lives: the workplace, the community, and the home. *Workplace Plus* integrates the CASAS life skill competencies and the SCANS Competencies and Foundation Skills with a complete civics and language syllabus and relevant social language.

Communicative competence in English is of critical importance in achieving self-sufficiency. *Workplace Plus* applies the best of current second language acquisition research to ensure immediate survival, rapidly enabling learners to:
- understand spoken and written general and employment-related language
- communicate in their <u>own</u> words
- understand the culture and civic expectations of their new environment and workplace
- cope with authentic documents they will encounter in their daily lives.

In order to achieve these goals with efficiency and speed, *Workplace Plus* weaves together four integrated strands: workplace skills, language, life skills, and civics.

Course length

Workplace Plus is designed to be used in a period of 60 to 90 classroom hours. This period can be shortened or lengthened, based on the needs of the group or the program. The Teacher's Edition gives detailed instructions for tailoring *Workplace Plus* to specific settings, circumstances, and student groups.

Components
Student's Book
The *Workplace Plus* Student's Book is a complete four-skill text, integrating listening, speaking, reading, and writing with workplace skills and life skills. The book contains 10 units, each one followed by a concise four-skill review section. For lesson planning and compliance with curriculum guidelines, the Scope and Sequence chart (on pages iv-vii) clearly spells out the following elements for each unit:
- workplace skills
- life skills
- civics concepts
- social language
- grammar
- SCANS Competencies and Foundation Skills

In order to facilitate student-centered instruction, *Workplace Plus* uses a variety of grouping strategies: pairs, groups, and whole class. In numerous activities, learners work with others to create a joint product. Those activities are labeled collaborative activities.

Two special features of the *Workplace Plus* Student's Book are <u>Do it yourself!</u> and <u>Authentic practice</u>.
   Because learners have an immediate need to use their new language outside the class, <u>Do it yourself!</u> provides a daily opportunity for students of diverse abilities to put new language into their own words. This affords them a chance

---

* *Literacy Plus*, which precedes *Workplace Plus 1*, serves the combined ESL, literacy, and civics needs of the pre-literate beginner.

to "try their wings" in the safe and supportive environment of the classroom.

Authentic practice activities create a "living language laboratory" within the classroom. Learners practice responding to authentic models of spoken and written English with the limited language they know. In this way, students build their confidence and skill in coping with the language of the real world.

Audiocassettes

Because listening comprehension is a fundamental survival and success skill for new speakers of English, *Workplace Plus* includes a comprehensive listening strand in each unit of the Student's Book. In addition to listening comprehension activities, there are numerous other opportunities for learners to practice their listening skills. All exercises that appear on audiocassette are marked with a 🎧 symbol. A transcript of each listening comprehension activity is located on its corresponding Teacher's Edition page, for easy reference.

Teacher's Edition

An interleaved Teacher's Edition provides page-by-page teaching suggestions that add value to the Student's Book. In addition to general and day-by-day teaching suggestions, each teacher's page includes optional activities, challenge activities, and language and culture / civics notes that will help teachers demystify and explain new language and culture concepts to students. Answers to all exercises and the tapescript of each listening comprehension activity are also readily found on all pages.

Workbook

In addition to the ample opportunities for reading and writing practice contained in the Student's Book, the *Workplace Plus* Workbook contains further reading and writing exercises. The Workbook is valuable for homework or for in-class activities. An added feature is a test preparation activity for each unit, with CASAS-like and BEST Test-like items which ensure that learners can "bubble in" and cope with the formats of standardized language tests.

Teacher's Resource Binder

A three-ring binder contains a wealth of valuable items to enable busy teachers to customize their instruction and make the preparation of supplementary teaching aids unnecessary. The Classroom Booster Pack provided with the Binder features pair-work cards, vocabulary flash cards, grammar self-checks, photo chat cards, and extension activities for daily use. Correlations of *Workplace Plus* with state and federal standards are also included in the Binder.

The following additional teacher-support materials are also available: Student Progress Checklists, Pre- and Post-Tests and Achievement Tests, Skills for Test Taking, and industry-specific Job Packs that are correlated with Student's Books 1 and 2.

Placement Test

A simple-to-administer test places students accurately within the *Workplace Plus* series.

Workplace Plus Companion Website

The *Workplace Plus* companion website (www.longman.com/workplaceplus)

provides numerous additional resources for students and teachers. This no-cost, high-benefit feature includes opportunities for further practice of language and content from the *Workplace Plus* Student's Book. For the teacher, there are optional strategies and materials that amplify the *Workplace Plus* Teacher's Edition.

Student's Book unit contents

Each unit in the *Workplace Plus* Student's Book uses an integrated three-step approach.

1. Practical conversations with integrated vocabulary

   Simple, memorable model conversations that are transferable to learners' own lives permit intensive practice of new vocabulary and key social language. These are followed by lively pair-work activities.

2. Practical grammar

   Essential grammatical structure practice enables learners to manipulate the vocabulary and practical conversations to express ideas of their own.

3. Authentic practice

   An entertaining picture story illustrates the authentic use of spoken target language and leads to a series of interactive comprehension tasks that help students cope with spoken language in the world outside the classroom.

A unique real-world reading enables students to understand culture and civics concepts of their new community and workplace. Then a series of authentic documents provides preparation for coping with the real documents students will encounter in the world outside the classroom.

Review

Following each unit is a three-page, four-skill review for learners to check their progress.

About the author and series advisor

Author

Joan Saslow

Joan Saslow has taught English as a second language and English as a foreign language to adults and young adults in the United States and Chile. She taught workplace English at the General Motors auto assembly plant in Tarrytown, NY; and Adult ESL at Westchester Community College and at Marymount College in New York. In addition, Ms. Saslow taught English and French at the Binational Centers of Valparaíso and Viña del Mar, Chile, and the Catholic University of Valparaíso.

Ms. Saslow is the series director of Longman's popular five-level adult series *True Colors, an EFL Course for Real Communication* and of *True Voices*, a five-level video course. She is the author of *Literacy Plus*, a two-level series that teaches beginning literacy, survival English, and essential civics concepts to adult pre-literate immigrants. She is also author of *English in Context: Reading Comprehension for Science and Technology*, a three-level series for English for special purposes. In addition, Ms. Saslow has been an editor of language teaching materials, a teacher trainer, and a frequent speaker at gatherings of ESL and EFL teachers for over thirty years.

Series advisor

Edwina Hoffman

Edwina Hoffman has taught English for speakers of other languages in South Florida and at the Miccosukee Tribe of Indians, and English as a foreign language in Venezuela. She provided teacher training in a seven-state area for federally funded multi-functional resource centers serving the southeastern part of the United States. Dr. Hoffman taught English composition at Florida International University and graduate ESOL methods at the University of Miami.

Dr. Hoffman is an instructional supervisor with the adult and vocational programs of Miami-Dade County Public Schools in Miami, Florida. She has acted as a consultant, reviewer, and author of adult ESOL materials for over twenty years. A graduate of Middlebury College, Dr. Hoffman's doctoral degree is from Florida International University.

3 Workplace Plus

Living and Working in English

Your life and work

Preview

Warm up. How do you start a conversation with someone you don't know?

Unit 1 objectives

- Start a conversation with someone you don't know.
- Get to know someone.
- Ask someone for a letter of recommendation.
- Talk about your skills, likes, and dislikes.
- Practice a job interview.
- Fill out an employment application.

Practical conversations

🎧 **A.** Listen and read.

A: Nice weather today.

B: Yes, it is. Beautiful.

A: You know, I don't think we've met. I'm Melanie Soto. I work on the third floor.

B: Nice to meet you, Melanie. I'm Luis Cruz.

A: Nice to meet you too. By the way, I like your tie.

B: You do? Thanks!

🎧 **B.** Listen again and repeat.

🎧 **Vocabulary**

Good weather adjectives	Bad weather adjectives

nice	awful
beautiful	terrible
gorgeous	horrible
Add your <u>own</u>: _____	Add your <u>own</u>: _____

C. Pair work. **Meet someone new. Make small talk. Use your <u>own</u> words.**

A: _____ weather today.

B: Yes, it is. _____.

A: You know, I don't think we've met. I'm _____.

B: Nice to meet you, _____. I'm _____.

A: _____. By the way, I like your _____.

B: You do? Thanks.

A. Listen and read.

A: How long have you been working here?
B: Not long. About a month.
A: Where did you work before that?
B: At Flushing Plumbing Supply.
A: That's incredible! So did I.
B: Wow. It's a small world!

B. Listen again and repeat.

Vocabulary

Ways to express surprise
That's incredible!
That's amazing!
You're kidding!
Add your <u>own</u>: _____

C. Pair work. Get to know a classmate. Use ideas from the box or your <u>own</u> idea.

working here	living in the U.S.	studying English

A: How long have you been _____?
B: _____.
A: Where did you _____ before that?
B: _____.
A: _____.

➤ Do it yourself!

Pair work. Begin a conversation. Make small talk. Use your <u>own</u> words and ideas.

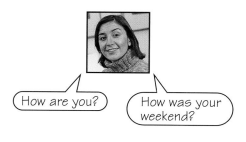

How are you?   How was your weekend?

Long time, no see!

I don't think we've met.

Practical conversations

A. Listen and read.

A: Could you do me a favor?

B: Of course. What is it?

A: Well, I'm applying for a job as a baby-sitter, and I need a reference. Would you mind writing me a letter of recommendation?

B: Not at all. I'd be glad to.

A: Thanks so much. I appreciate it.

B. Listen again and repeat.

To whom it may concern:

Fran Lin has been my student for two years. She is a good worker and is always on time. I can recommend Ms. Lin

Vocabulary

Occupations

a mechanic   an engineer   a plumber   an office manager   a bank teller

Add your <u>own</u>: _____

C. Pair work. Ask for a reference. Use one of the occupations from the vocabulary or use your <u>own</u> occupation.

A: Could you do me a favor?

B: _____. What is it?

A: Well, I'm applying for a job as _____, and I need a reference. Would you mind writing me a letter of recommendation?

B: Not at all. I'd be glad to.

A: _____.

A. Listen and read.

A: So tell me something about yourself.

B: Well, I really enjoy working with my hands. I'm pretty good at that.

A: What about cooking?

B: Actually, I like cooking, but I'm not very good at it.

B. Listen again and repeat.

Vocabulary

Skills

| driving | fixing cars | working with children | working with people | using a computer |

Add your own: _____

C. Pair work. Discuss your likes and dislikes. Use the vocabulary and the words in the box.

| love | like | enjoy | don't mind | dislike | hate | can't stand |
| **+** | | | | | | **–** |

A: So tell me something about yourself.

B: Well, I really enjoy _____. I'm pretty good at that.

A: What about _____?

B: Actually, I _____.

> **Do it yourself!**

Pair work. Create a conversation for the people in the picture. Say as much as you can.

➤ Practical grammar

The present perfect continuous

Use the present perfect continuous with <u>for</u> or <u>since</u> to describe activities that began in the past and continue in the present.

I've been working here **for** two months.

Form the present perfect continuous with <u>have been</u> or <u>has been</u> and the continuous (<u>-ing</u>) form of the verb.

She**'s been talking** on the phone **since** 10:00.

Has Martin **been living** here long? Yes, he has. Since 1999.

Where **has** he **been working**? At Micro-tech.

Use **for** with amounts of time: for six years.

Use **since** with specific times and dates: since we met, since May.

A. Complete the sentences. Fill in the ovals.

1. How long _____ that telephone call?
   - ⓐ have you been waiting for
   - ⓑ you are waiting for
   - ⓒ you waited for

2. We _____ three hours.
   - ⓐ waited since
   - ⓑ have been waiting for
   - ⓒ waiting for

3. How long _____?
   - ⓐ it has been raining
   - ⓑ has it been raining
   - ⓒ it's raining

4. It _____ Tuesday.
   - ⓐ has been raining for
   - ⓑ been raining since
   - ⓒ has been raining since

B. Write questions with the words. Use the present perfect continuous.

1. How long / you / live / in this city?

   How long have you been living in this city?

2. Ellen / work here / longer than Terry?

   _____

3. you / take care of children / a long time?

   _____

4. What / you / do / I saw you?

   _____

C. **Learn about your classmates' lives and work. Write two questions to ask a classmate. Use the present perfect continuous. Use a question mark (?).**

1. _____

2. _____

Gerunds for describing likes, dislikes, and skills

Describe your likes and dislikes with gerunds.	Describe your skills with gerunds.

I like **working** with people.

That's great. We have a good job at the Holiday Hotel.

Tell me something about your skills.

Well, I'm great at **fixing** old cars.

D. **Complete each sentence with a gerund.**

1. I'm good at _organizing_. I enjoy _____ an administrative assistant.
   (organize)   (be)

2. I don't mind _____ the coffee maker, and you won't have to pay me!
               (repair)

3. I'm looking for a job as a receptionist. I'm good at _____ with people.
                                                        (work)

4. I really dislike _____ dirty. I'd rather not work in a garage.
                    (get)

See page 150 for spelling rules for the gerund.

➤ Do it yourself!

A. **Personalization. Use gerunds to describe your strengths and weaknesses and your likes and dislikes.**

Strengths: *I'm good at*	Weaknesses: *I'm not good at*	Likes: *I like*	Dislikes: *I don't like*

B. **Discussion. Talk about your chart with a group.**

Authentic practice

A. Read and listen again. Then check <u>True</u>, <u>False</u>, or <u>Maybe</u>.

	True	False	Maybe
1. Mr. Han and Ms. Ramos have been working together for three years.	☐	☐	☐
2. Ms. Ramos's first name is Diana.	☐	☐	☐
3. Ms. Ramos speaks English at A-Mart.	☐	☐	☐
4. Ms. Ramos doesn't want to fill out a questionnaire.	☐	☐	☐

B. Listen. Underline <u>your</u> response.

1. **YOU** Not at all.   **YOU** Not long.

2. **YOU** My supervisor told me about it.   **YOU** It's a small world.

3. **YOU** Of course.   **YOU** I appreciate it.

C. Listen again. Read <u>your</u> response out loud.

🎧 **A.** Listening comprehension. **Listen to the job interview with a bus driver. Then listen again and check the things Mr. Witherspoon likes, doesn't mind, doesn't like, or hates.**

	Likes	Doesn't mind	Doesn't like	Hates
1. being late	☐	☐	☐	☐
2. waiting	☐	☐	☐	☐
3. being formal	☐	☐	☐	☐
4. working at Greenmont Bus Company	☐	☐	☐	☐
5. getting up early	☐	☐	☐	☐

🎧 **B.** Listen again and write **True** or **False**.

1. _____ Mr. Witherspoon has been waiting for a long time.

2. _____ The receptionist was there when Mr. Witherspoon entered.

3. _____ Mr. Witherspoon has been working at Greenmont Bus since February.

4. _____ The Witherspoons had a baby in December.

C. True story. **Tell your partner about a job interview you or a friend had. Use words from the box or your own ideas.**

a job application   a job   references   a letter of recommendation   an ad

➤ Do it yourself!

A. Write your **own** response. **Then read your interview out loud with a partner.**

Hi. I'm Sara Molina. Please call me Sara. What would you like me to call you?

YOU _____

Please tell me a little bit about yourself.

YOU _____

Well, we have several openings right now. When can you give me a list of references?

YOU _____

B. Culture talk. **In the country you come from, what are the customs about using first names? Compare cultures with your classmates.**

Authentic practice

Do's and don'ts for job interviews

A. Read and listen to the letters.

Ask Joan
Culture tips for newcomers

Dear Joan:
I've been living in this country for two years, and I've been taking care of children in my home since I got here. I love working with children, and I'd like to have a full-time job outside the home in a day-care center. I'm writing because I have an interview next week at an employment agency. Joan, this is my first job interview! Any tips for me?

Irene from Moline

Dear Irene:
It sounds like you have great experience for that day-care position. I have only a couple of suggestions. Wear simple, neat clothes. Don't wear a lot of makeup or strong perfume—lots of people don't like that. Bring your references with you. Oh, and just be yourself. I'm sure you'll get the job. Best of luck!

Joan

Dear Joan:
I was an accountant in my country, but I've been driving a taxi since I got here last year. I've also been studying English, and I think I'm ready to start looking for office work while I study for my accountant's license. Do you have any advice for me?

Arturo the accountant

Dear Arturo:
You've learned enough English in one year to restart your career. That's pretty amazing! Congratulations! Be sure to dress neatly and conservatively. Tell the interviewer about your skills and experience. Avoid doing things that might annoy people, like arriving late or chewing gum.

Joan

B. Check <u>Irene</u> or <u>Arturo</u>.

	Irene	Arturo
1. has been driving a taxi	❏	❏
2. has been studying English	❏	❏
3. has been living here for two years	❏	❏
4. has been taking care of children	❏	❏

C. **What does Joan suggest for job interviews? Write each phrase in the correct column.**

chewing gum	wearing strong perfume
bringing your references	being yourself
being neat	wearing simple, neat clothes
wearing a lot of makeup	being on time

Joan suggests	**Joan advises against**
_____	_____
_____	_____
_____	_____
_____	_____

A pre-employment application

Read the pre-employment application and fill it out for yourself.

Town of Buenavista, Oklahoma
2600 North Main
Buenavista, OK 73129

PRE-EMPLOYMENT APPLICATION

Date of application: _____

_____
Applicant's name
_____
Current mailing address

Are you currently employed? [circle one] **Y / N**   If yes, position: _____

Employer and address: _____

How long have you been working for this employer? _____

If not currently employed, last position held: _____

Dates: from _____ to _____

Describe the type of position you are seeking: _____
_____

Please list your skills (Examples: **driving, repairing equipment, speaking another language, etc.**).
_____

➤ Do it yourself!   A plan-ahead project

A. **Bring in job applications from places such as a supermarket, bank, discount store, or convenience store, or use the one on pages 151 and 152. Fill out an application.**

B. **Pair work. Practice a job interview with a classmate. Use the applications.**

Review

A. **Pair work or group work.**

- Where are the people?
- What do they want?

Ask and answer questions.

Create conversations.

Tell a story.

Say as much as you can.

	Likes	Doesn't like
1. driving	☐	☐
2. getting up in the middle of the night	☐	☐
3. doing paperwork	☐	☐
4. working with a lot of people	☐	☐

C. Choose **your** response. Fill in the ovals.

1. "I like that jacket."

   ⓐ It's a small world.   ⓑ Thanks.

2. "Would you mind driving my daughter to school?"

   ⓐ Not at all.   ⓑ Do you like driving?

3. "Tell me something about yourself. What do you enjoy doing?"

   ⓐ I haven't been doing that for long.   ⓑ Cooking.

D. Write responses to the interviewer.

1. **Interviewer:** I'm Eduardo Trent. Do you mind if I call you by your first name?

   YOU _____

2. **Interviewer:** Please tell me something about yourself.

   YOU _____

3. **Interviewer:** Could I see your references?

   YOU _____

E. Write questions with the words. Use the present perfect continuous.

1. How long / you / study English?

   _____

2. What / he / do / 1999?

   _____

3. Who / work here / the longest?

   _____

4. you / wait / long?

   _____

F. Complete the paragraph with gerunds.

Juan Sepulveda was a pharmacist in his country. Right now he's looking for a part-time job so he can study English and get ready for his licensing exam. He likes _____ and _____, and he likes _____ at night
            1. cook   2. clean   3. work

because his English classes are in the afternoon. He doesn't enjoy _____
                                                         4. drive

and he's not too good at _____ office machines, but he doesn't mind
                                  5. fix

_____ other kinds of office work. Two things he hates _____
            6. do   7. do

are handling cash and _____ children.
                       8. take care of

G. Fill out the job application for yourself.

Stilton Hotel Corporation
2201 Broadway
Cabo Maria, FL 32862   **APPLICATION FOR EMPLOYMENT**

_____
Name and current mailing address

_____
Current employer and address

If not currently employed, last employment: _____
                                                        Employer

_____   _____
              Address   Dates (from – to)

Skills: _____

H. Composition. On a separate sheet of paper, write about the picture on page 12. Say as much as you can.

Now I can
❑ start a conversation with someone I don't know.
❑ get to know someone.
❑ ask someone for a letter of recommendation.
❑ talk about my skills, likes, and dislikes.
❑ have a job interview.
❑ fill out an employment application.
❑ _____.

Your environment

 Preview

Warm up. What time should the guests arrive?

A dinner party!
Time: 6:30
Date: May 11
Place: 35 Grove Street
RSVP: 929-3430

Hope you can come!
Marian

Unit 2 objectives

- Extend and accept an invitation and make plans to meet.
- Ask for and give directions within a building.
- Ask for and give assistance on an elevator.
- Use maps, plans, and building directories.
- Ask for and give directions for public transportation.

Model 1   Ask for and give directions within a building.

🎧 **A. Listen and read.**

A: Excuse me. Can you tell me how to get to the parking garage?

B: Sure. It's on the third floor. Take either the elevator or the escalator to the second floor. Walk to the end of the hall and then go up the stairs.

A: Thanks.

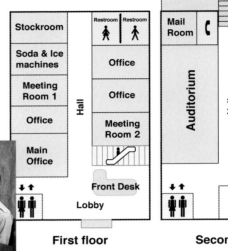

🎧 **B. Listen again and repeat.**

🎧 **Vocabulary**

Directions

Go straight.

Turn right *or* Make a right.

Make your second left.

Go down the hall.

Go to the end of the hall.

Walk down the stairs.

Take the escalator.

Take the elevator.

C. Pair work. Ask for and give directions to places on the building diagram above. Use the vocabulary and your <u>own</u> choices.

A: _____. Can you tell me how to get to _____?

B: _____. It's on the _____ floor. _____.

A: Thanks.

A. **Listen and read.**

> **A:** Hold the elevator, please! Going up?
> **B:** Yes. Where are you going?
> **A:** Two, please.
> **B:** There you go.
> **A:** Thanks.

B. **Listen again and repeat.**

Vocabulary

Building interiors

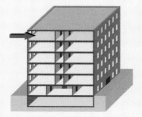   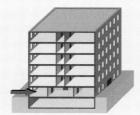   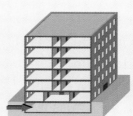   

On the top floor.   On the first (or ground) floor.   In the basement.   In Room 122.

C. **Pair work. Choose a place in the Brimstone Building. Share an elevator ride up or down. Use the vocabulary and the building directory.**

> **A:** Hold the elevator, please! Going _____?
> **B:** Yes. Where are you going?
> **A:** _____, please.
> **B:** There you go.
> **A:** _____.

THE BRIMSTONE BUILDING

Executive Offices	Ground floor
Benefits Department	110
Human Resources Office	211
General Manager's Office	212
Medical Services	313
Records Department	Basement

➤ Do it yourself!

A. Collaborative activity. **Make a diagram or a building directory on the chalkboard.**

B. Discussion. **Take turns giving directions to places on the diagram or the directory.**

Practical conversations

A. Listen and read.

A: Hello. Ben's Warehouse.

B: Hello. Could you please tell me how to get there? I'm taking the bus.

A: Where are you now?

B: At the corner of Fulton and Redwood.

A: Well, take the number 6 to Hunter Street and transfer there to the 1.

B: OK. And where do I get off?

A: Get off at Elm. The warehouse is right on the corner. You can't miss it.

B. Listen again and repeat.

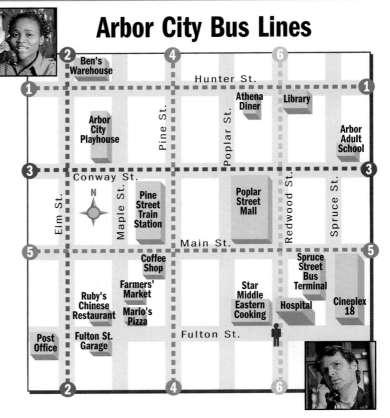

Arbor City Bus Lines

Vocabulary

Directions

It's on Main Street.

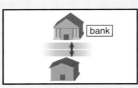

It's across from the bank.

It's between the bank and the school. It's next to the bank.

C. Pair work. Get directions from Arbor Adult School to the post office and the hospital.

A: _____.

B: _____. Could you please tell me how to get there? I'm taking the bus.

A: Where are you now?

B: At _____.

A: Well, take the number _____ to _____ and transfer there to the _____.

B: OK. And where do I get off?

A: Get off at _____. The _____ is _____. You can't miss it.

18   Unit 2

A. Listen and read.

A: I was wondering. Would you like to have coffee with us sometime?

B: We'd love to. When would be good?

A: How about Saturday afternoon? . . . Around 2:00?

B: That's fine. Where should we meet?

A: Why don't we meet at the coffee shop on Main? It's right across the street from the train station.

B. Listen again and repeat.

Ways to accept an invitation

| We'd love to. | Sounds great. |
| That would be nice. | Yes. Let's do that! |

Vocabulary

Social activities

go to the movies   go out to eat   go for a walk   go shopping

C. Pair work. Make plans to meet in Arbor City. Use the map on page 18.

A: I was wondering. Would you like to _____ with _____ sometime?

B: _____. When would be good?

A: How about _____? . . . Around _____?

B: _____. Where should we meet?

A: Why don't we meet at _____? It's _____.

➤ Do it yourself!

A. Personalization. Complete the chart with activities and places in your town.

Activity	Place	Location
go to the movies	Metroplex	at the corner of State and First

B. Pair work. Give your partner directions. You can walk, drive, or take the bus.

➤ Practical grammar

Directions, warnings, requests, and suggestions

Use imperatives to give instructions or directions.

    Take the number 7 bus to Elm Street.

Use imperatives to give warnings.

    The fire alarm rang. **Don't take** the elevator.

Use imperatives with <u>please</u> for polite requests and written invitations.

    Please bring me the map. (*or* **Bring** me the map, **please**.)

    Please join us for dinner at the Athena Diner for Martha's birthday.

Make suggestions and express invitations with <u>Let's</u>, <u>Let's</u> <u>not</u>, and <u>Why</u> <u>don't</u> . . . ?

    Let's take the bus. **Let's not drive**.

    Why don't we **meet** at 2:00 in the break room?

A. **Read what each person says. Then respond with a direction or a warning, or make a suggestion.**

1. "I don't like my new job."

    (YOU) _____

2. "Where should we have the meeting?"

    (YOU) _____

3. "I'd like to see that new movie at the Metroplex."

    (YOU) _____

4. "I'm hungry."

    (YOU) _____

Indirect commands

Use <u>ask</u> or <u>tell</u> plus an infinitive to give directions to other people. An infinitive is <u>to</u> plus a verb.

                        infinitive

Janet: Laura, please **ask Pete to call** me later.

Laura: OK . . . . Pete, please call Janet later.

B. Continue each person's speech with an indirect command. Use <u>ask</u> or <u>tell</u> and an infinitive.

1. I need some clean mops. *Please ask Mariana to get me some mops from the supply room.*

   Mariana / get me some mops / from the supply room

2. Bill needs directions to the office from the warehouse. _____

   _____

   him / walk to the corner of Grand and Third and turn left

3. There's a big spill in the work area. _____

   _____

   the maintenance staff / clean it up fast

4. The Costas want to have dinner with us at the new Brazilian restaurant. _____

   _____

   them / meet us there at 7:30

5. John has to pick up the car at 5:00. _____

   _____

   him / not / forget

➤ Do it yourself!

Form groups of three students. Partner A: Tell Partner B to tell Partner C how to get to your house or to another place in your town.

Take the number 6 bus to Central Avenue. Get off and turn right on Central. Walk two blocks. I'm at 63 Central Avenue. See you and Mark later, OK?

OK!

LATER

Hey, Mark, take the number 6 to Central Avenue. Turn right on Central and go to number 63. It's two blocks.

OK. Great.

🎧 **A. Read and listen again. Then choose an answer to each question. Fill in the ovals.**

1. Who needs directions?

   ⓐ Pete.

   ⓑ Ms. Benson.

2. Where's Ms. Benson's house?

   ⓐ In Arbor City.

   ⓑ On Maple Street.

3. What is the house near?

   ⓐ The school.

   ⓑ Make your second left.

🎧 **B. Listen. Underline your response.**

1. **YOU** The corner of Fulton and Elm.   **YOU** I'm taking the bus.

2. **YOU** You can't miss it.   **YOU** OK.

3. **YOU** At the Smith Street stop.   **YOU** We'd love to.

🎧 **C. Listen again. Read your response out loud.**

🎧 **A. Listening comprehension. Listen to the conversation. Then listen again and check True, False, or Maybe.**

	True	False	Maybe
1. The man wanted to go to the fourth floor.	❑	❑	❑
2. The fourth floor is the top floor.	❑	❑	❑
3. The woman in the elevator was going to the fourth floor.	❑	❑	❑
4. The man is a karate teacher.	❑	❑	❑

🎧 **B. Listen again and put the events in order.**

1. _____ He goes to the fourth floor.
2. _____ The elevator goes up.
3. _1_ The man gets on the elevator.
4. _____ The elevator goes down.
5. _____ He gets off the elevator.

C. True story. Did you ever have a difficult time finding a place? What happened? Use the ideas in the box or your own idea. Tell the story to your partner.

reading a map

understanding directions

losing directions

➤ Do it yourself!

A. Write your own response. Then read your conversation out loud with a partner.

I just realized I have no idea how to get to your place. Can you give me directions?

YOU _____

Please give me directions from the school.

YOU _____

Great. Thanks. Would you mind giving me the number of your house again?

YOU _____

B. Culture talk. In the country you come from, what is elevator etiquette? Compare cultures with your classmates.

Elevator etiquette and social etiquette

🎧 **A.** Read and listen to the letters.

Ask Joan
Culture tips for newcomers

Dear Joan:
I don't understand something that happened to me today. In the elevator at work this morning, the other people in the elevator looked at me and then moved away from me. I get the feeling I did something wrong, but I don't know what it was.

Otis Schindler

Dear Otis:
You don't give me much information, so let me tell you some of the "unwritten rules" of elevator etiquette. First of all, face front. Second, if there are only a few people in the elevator, don't stand too near any of the other passengers. It makes people very uncomfortable. And if the floor buttons are only on one side of the car and you're standing in front of them, offer to press buttons for passengers on the other side of the car. The simplest way to do this is to say, "What floor?" or "Where are you going?" If someone asks *you* that question, answer with a floor number, not the name of the place you are going to.

That should do it!

Joan

Dear Joan:
Last week a co-worker invited me to a party at her house. I'm very nervous about the party. First of all, in my religion we don't drink alcoholic beverages, and I think many people drink alcohol here. Is it rude or unfriendly to ask for a nonalcoholic drink? Also, the invitation is for 6 o'clock. In my country, we never get to a party at the exact time of the invitation — we get there later. Please tell me what to do. Hurry, Joan. The party is this Sunday!

Nervous Nadia

Dear Nadia:
You can stop worrying. Your co-worker will offer a variety of beverages. Many people in this country don't drink alcoholic beverages either, so when your host offers a drink, just ask for fruit juice or soda. No one will think that's unusual. You didn't say if the party was a dinner party. If the party is a sit-down dinner, and the invitation is for 6:00, it's impolite to arrive after about 6:15. Enjoy yourself, make new friends, and have fun!

Joan

B. Read Joan's advice again. Read the statements and check <u>True</u> or <u>False</u>.

	True	False
1. Don't stand very near people in an elevator.	☐	☐
2. Stand with your back to the door.	☐	☐
3. It's OK to ask for juice when some people are drinking alcohol.	☐	☐
4. It doesn't matter what time you arrive at a dinner party.	☐	☐

Paul wants to invite two co-workers, Tran and Nadia, to dinner at his house. Write directions for one of Paul's co-workers. Nadia is going to Paul's from home. Tran is going directly from the Luna Italian Restaurant. They can walk, drive, or take a bus.

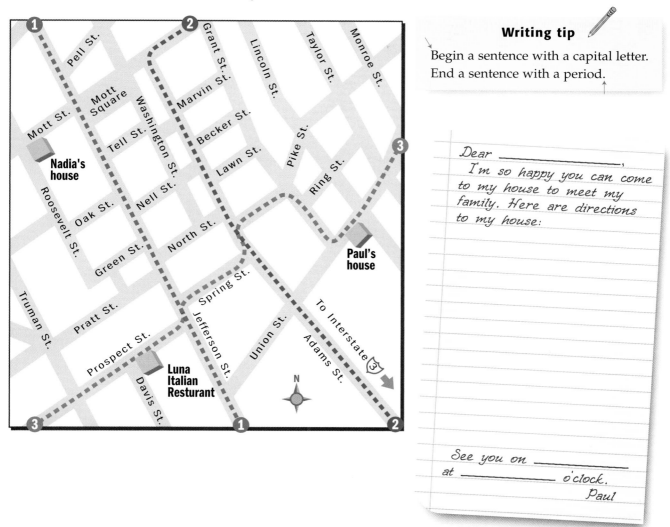

Writing tip ✏️

Begin a sentence with a capital letter.
End a sentence with a period.

Dear _____,
I'm so happy you can come to my house to meet my family. Here are directions to my house:

See you on _____
at _____ o'clock.
                    Paul

➤ **Do it yourself!**   A plan-ahead project

A. Bring in public transportation maps, town or city maps, or mall or building diagrams. Or use the one on page 153.

B. Discussion. Compare maps. Give directions to your classmates to places on the map.

Review

A. Pair work or group work.

- Where are the people?
- What are they doing?

Ask and answer questions.

Create conversations.

Tell a story.

Say as much as you can.

B. Listen to the conversation about instructions for the next day. Read the statements and listen again. Check the directions, warnings, and requests you hear.

1. ☐ Open the building early.
2. ☐ Close the building late.
3. ☐ Leave the keys on Ben's desk.
4. ☐ Check the cartons.
5. ☐ Put two cartons of detergent in Ben's office.
6. ☐ Check the labels on the detergent.
7. ☐ Don't put cheese on the sandwich.

C. Choose your response. Fill in the ovals.

1. "I was wondering, would you like to have coffee after work?"
   ⓐ Sure. When would be good?   ⓑ Sure. I don't know how to get there.

2. "Excuse me. Can you tell me how to get to the warehouse?"
   ⓐ Where are you now?   ⓑ Tell him to take the bus.

3. "You can't miss it."
   ⓐ Where are you going?   ⓑ Thanks. See you then.

4. "Why don't we meet in the break room?"
   ⓐ I don't know.   ⓑ That's fine.

D. Write directions from your house or apartment to your supermarket. Begin each new sentence with a capital letter. End each sentence with a period.

_____

_____

_____

E. Write a response to each statement or question. Use your own words.

1. "I was wondering. Where would you like to have the meeting?"
   (YOU) _____

2. "Hold the elevator, please!"
   (YOU) _____

3. "Why don't we meet at the Farmers' Market on Maple Street?"
   (YOU) _____

F. **Look at the building plan. Read the statements and check <u>True</u> or <u>False</u>.**

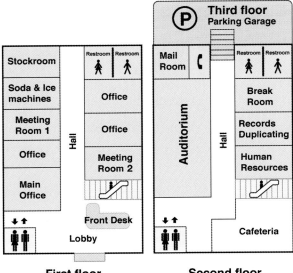

First floor   Second floor

	True	False
1. The main office is on the first floor.	❏	❏
2. The cafeteria is next to the parking garage.	❏	❏
3. The break room is down the hall from the stockroom.	❏	❏
4. Access to the parking garage is at the end of the first floor hall.	❏	❏
5. To get to the Human Resources department from the first floor, take the elevator or the escalator.	❏	❏

G. **Composition.** **On a separate sheet of paper, write about the picture on page 26. Say as much as you can.**

> **Now I can**
> ❏ extend and accept an invitation and make plans to meet.
> ❏ ask for and give directions within a building.
> ❏ ask for and give assistance on an elevator.
> ❏ use maps, plans, and building directories.
> ❏ ask for and give directions for public transportation.
> ❏ _____.

Your equipment and machines

 Preview

Warm up. What's a warranty?

MicroTastic®

Commercial Microwave Oven

Warranty

All warranty service is to be provided by
an authorized MicroTastic® technician.
For service, call 1-800-MTASTIC.

Length of warranty—MicroTastic® will replace or repair:

Full one-year: from date of purchase	Limited three-year: second through fourth year from date of purchase
Any part that fails because of a defect in materials or workmanship. During this one-year period, all parts and labor will be provided free of charge.	The magnetron tube, if it fails because of a defect in materials or workmanship. During this period, purchaser will be responsible for costs of labor.

Unit 3 objectives

- Read and understand a product warranty.
- Admit a possible error.
- Reassure someone.
- Express frustration with equipment malfunctions.
- Troubleshoot a problem.

Model 1   Discuss a warranty.

🎧 **A. Listen and read.**

> **A:** I wonder if this freezer is still under warranty.
> **B:** When was it purchased?
> **A:** About six months ago.
> **B:** No problem. It has a one-year warranty on parts and labor.

🎧 **B. Listen again and repeat.**

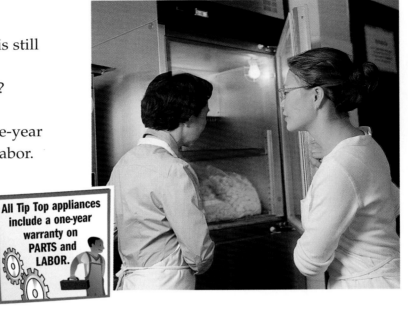

All Tip Top appliances include a one-year warranty on PARTS and LABOR.

🎧 **Vocabulary**

Equipment and machines

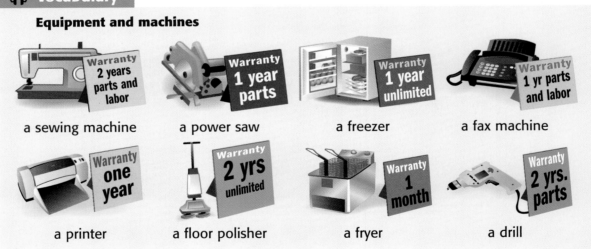

Warranty 2 years parts and labor — a sewing machine

Warranty 1 year parts — a power saw

Warranty 1 year unlimited — a freezer

Warranty 1 yr parts and labor — a fax machine

Warranty one year — a printer

Warranty 2 yrs unlimited — a floor polisher

Warranty 1 month — a fryer

Warranty 2 yrs. parts — a drill

C. Pair work. Discuss a warranty. Use the vocabulary or your <u>own</u> machines and warranties.

> **A:** I wonder if this _____ is still under warranty.
> **B:** When was it purchased?
> **A:** _____.
> **B:** _____. It has _____ warranty.

A. Listen and read.

A: Uh-oh. I'm going to get in trouble.
B: What do you mean?
A: Well, I think I broke this sander.
B: Maybe you'd better tell someone.
A: I don't know. They'll think it's my fault.
B: Don't worry. It's always good to speak up.

B. Listen again and repeat.

Vocabulary

What to do when something is broken

| call the manager | call the help line | call maintenance | ask someone for help |

C. Pair work. Express concern about breaking something. Talk about what to do. Use these machines or the ones on page 30. Or use your <u>own</u> machines.

A: Uh-oh. I'm going to get in trouble.
B: What do you mean?
A: Well, I think I broke _____.
B: Maybe you'd better _____.
A: I don't know. They'll think it's my fault.
B: Don't worry. It's always good to speak up.

➤ Do it yourself!

A. Personalization. Complete the chart with machines or equipment you have, or a friend has.

Machine	New / Used		Warranty?	Terms
my car	☐	☑	☑	6 months or 3000 miles
1.	☐	☐	☐	
2.	☐	☐	☐	

B. Discussion. Talk about the information on your chart.

Practical conversations

A. Listen and read.

A: Can you believe it? This hose is clogged again.

B: You're kidding. When was it serviced?

A: Just last week.

B: That's ridiculous. What a waste of time!

A: You can say that again! Let's write up a repair or replace order.

B. Listen again and repeat.

Machine maintenance

serviced
cleaned
fixed

Repair or Replace Order

☑ Check after 3 services in 3-month period.

Date serviced
3/15
5/2
5/10

Vocabulary

Mechanical problems

| clogged | stuck | jammed | out of service |

C. Pair work. Decide to write up a repair or replace order. Use these machines and equipment or your <u>own</u> machines and equipment.

| copier | sink | sewing machine | toilet | vacuum cleaner |

A: Can you believe it? The _____ is _____ again.

B: You're kidding. When was it _____?

A: _____.

B: That's ridiculous. What a waste of time!

A: _____. Let's write up a repair or replace order.

🎧 **A. Listen and read.**

> **A:** What's the matter?
> **B:** My computer crashed. And I need to order supplies.
> **A:** Did you try restarting it?
> **B:** Yes, I did. But that didn't help.
> **A:** Maybe you'd better tell someone.

🎧 **B. Listen again and repeat.**

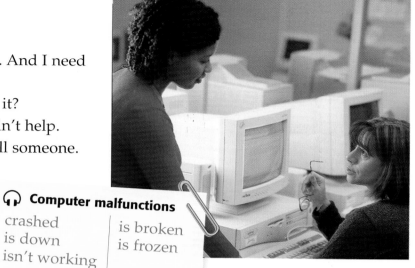

🎧 **Computer malfunctions**

crashed	is broken
is down	is frozen
isn't working	

🎧 **Vocabulary**

Computer activities

File Folders
Price: $13.99
Unit: 100/box   ORDER

detergent ..... 3 cartons
paper towels .... 15 rolls
cleanser .... 2 boxes

Aircraft   T- 343
Dep. Time   06:45pm
Arr. Time   08:17pm
Total Stops   None
Aircraft   MP267
Dep. Time   07:00am
Arr. Time   09:37am
Total Stops   None

Starlight Diner
Hamburger plate   4.95
Salad   2.95
Coffee   .80
                                .61
Tax $9.31
Total
Thank you!

Ace Elect
Memo
To: Edward Stone
From: Miriam Yu
CC: Anita Cordova
Date: 5/11/03
Re: New stock ro

order supplies	check stock	make reservations	print receipts	write memos

C. **Pair work. Discuss a computer problem. Use activities from the vocabulary or your own computer activities.**

> **A:** What's the matter?
> **B:** My computer _____. And I need to _____.
> **A:** Did you try restarting it?
> **B:** Yes, I did. But that didn't help.
> **A:** Well, maybe you'd better _____.

➤ **Do it yourself!**

A. **Pair work. Complete the chart about problems with two of your machines.**

B. **Discussion. Talk about what you did when a machine malfunctioned.**

Machine	sticks	clogs	jams	crashes
my camera	☐	☐	☑	☐
1.	☐	☐	☐	☐
2.	☐	☐	☐	☐

➤ Practical grammar

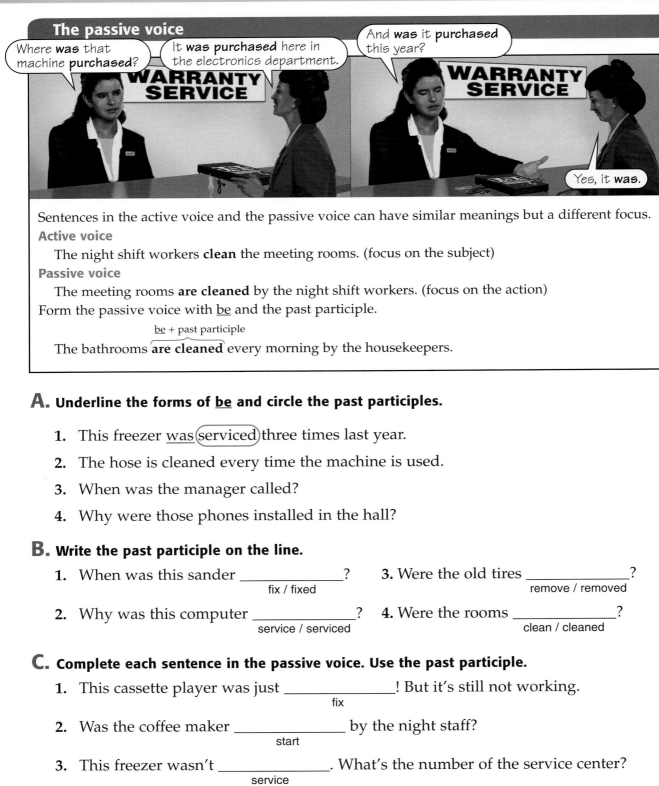

Sentences in the active voice and the passive voice can have similar meanings but a different focus.

Active voice

The night shift workers **clean** the meeting rooms. (focus on the subject)

Passive voice

The meeting rooms **are cleaned** by the night shift workers. (focus on the action)

Form the passive voice with <u>be</u> and the past participle.

$$\overbrace{}^{\underline{be}\ +\ past\ participle}$$

The bathrooms **are cleaned** every morning by the housekeepers.

A. Underline the forms of <u>be</u> and circle the past participles.

1. This freezer <u>was</u> (serviced) three times last year.

2. The hose is cleaned every time the machine is used.

3. When was the manager called?

4. Why were those phones installed in the hall?

B. Write the past participle on the line.

1. When was this sander _____?
   fix / fixed

2. Why was this computer _____?
   service / serviced

3. Were the old tires _____?
   remove / removed

4. Were the rooms _____?
   clean / cleaned

C. Complete each sentence in the passive voice. Use the past participle.

1. This cassette player was just _____! But it's still not working.
   fix

2. Was the coffee maker _____ by the night staff?
   start

3. This freezer wasn't _____. What's the number of the service center?
   service

4. The batteries were _____ yesterday, but now they're dead.
   replace

D. Complete each sentence in the passive voice.

1. **A:** When was the filter changed?
   B: It _____ last week.

2. **A:** Where was the truck purchased?
   B: It _____ at Trucks, Inc.

3. **A:** Was the thermostat adjusted?
   B: Yes, it _____ this morning.

4. **A:** Were the phones moved?
   B: Yes, they _____ by Ann.

Irregular past participles: Review

The following verbs have irregular past participles.

🎧 Verb	Simple past	Past participle	🎧 Verb	Simple past	Past participle
begin	began	**begun**	give	gave	**given**
break	broke	**broken**	make	made	**made**
bring	brought	**brought**	sell	sold	**sold**
buy	bought	**bought**	send	sent	**sent**
choose	chose	**chosen**	take	took	**taken**
drive	drove	**driven**	write	wrote	**written**

A more complete list of irregular past participles can be found on page 148.

E. Complete each sentence in the passive voice.

1. The repair or replace order _was written_ a week ago.
   <u>write</u>

2. Where _____ the car _____ for repairs last time?
   <u>bring</u>

3. When _____ this washing machine _____?
   <u>buy</u>

4. That floor polisher _____ not _____ the day before yesterday.
   <u>break</u>

➤ Do it yourself!

Pair work. Look at the service receipts for two cars. Compare what was done by Vinny's Car Repair and Maisie's Garage.

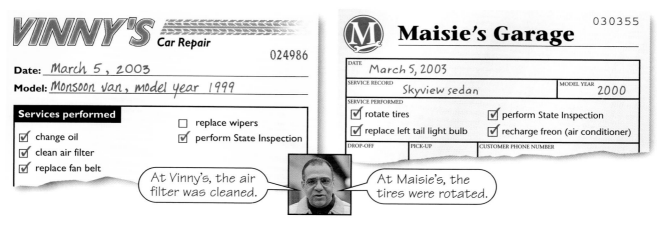

Authentic practice

A. Read and listen again. Then check <u>True</u>, <u>False</u>, or <u>Maybe</u>.

	True	False	Maybe
1. The wires were broken before.	☐	☐	☐
2. The cooks will reconnect the wires.	☐	☐	☐
3. The worker who broke the wires will speak up.	☐	☐	☐

B. Listen. Underline <u>your</u> response.

1. **YOU** Is it clogged?   **YOU** What do you mean?

2. **YOU** That's ridiculous.   **YOU** Now it won't work at all.

3. **YOU** What a waste of time.   **YOU** Great. Let's start now.

C. Listen again. Read <u>your</u> response out loud.

A. Listening comprehension. Listen to the conversation about a computer problem. Then listen again and check <u>True</u>, <u>False</u>, or <u>Maybe</u>.

	True	False	Maybe
1. The computer crashed.	☐	☐	☐
2. The computer was purchased at Electronics World.	☐	☐	☐
3. Holding down the control key helps for a while.	☐	☐	☐
4. The computer needs more memory.	☐	☐	☐

B. True story. Tell your partner about a machine or piece of equipment that was serviced or repaired.

I sent it to a service center.

I took it to a repair shop.

I fixed it myself.

➤ Do it yourself!

A. Write your <u>own</u> response. Then read your conversation out loud with a partner.

I'm definitely in big trouble now.

YOU _____

The hose was clogged. I disconnected it, but I forgot to turn off the machine. Now there's dirt all over the floor.

YOU _____

Maybe I should just say I found it like this when I got here. Then no one will know who made the mess.

YOU _____

B. Culture talk. In the country you come from, how do you tell a supervisor that you made a mistake? Compare cultures with your classmates.

Speak up about equipment breakdowns.

🎧 **A. Read and listen to the letters.**

Ask Joan
Culture tips for newcomers

Dear Joan:

I'm a cafeteria worker in a manufacturing plant. I like my job. I was hired only six months ago, and last week I was promoted! I have a problem, though, and I hope you can help me with it.

I am responsible for purchasing all supplies and preparing breakfast for the first shift. I come in early, and there's not much time to clean up and get ready. Sometimes I work too fast. When I try to clean under the burners, I sometimes disconnect the wires by mistake. This has already happened three times, and I'm afraid to tell the manager that I did it again today. She might think I'm not careful with the equipment.

I can't fix the wires myself, and I can't do all the cooking if I don't have all the burners working. What should I do? I don't want to get in trouble or lose my job.

I really need advice.

Laura

Dear Laura:

You have no idea how many letters like yours I receive! Many workers are afraid to tell their managers when something breaks. So instead of reporting a problem, workers often avoid working with the machine, probably hoping that someone else will solve the problem for them.

Remember: Managers want the work to get done. If you are having a problem with equipment, just speak up. Your manager will help you. She can probably show you how to clean under the burner without breaking the electrical connection. Don't worry. Your concern about the equipment will be rewarded, not blamed!

Joan

B. Choose an answer to each question. Fill in the ovals.

1. What's the problem?
   ⓐ A worker is afraid to speak up about a problem.   ⓑ The stove is dirty.

2. How often has this problem occurred?
   ⓐ Once.   ⓑ Several times.

3. What advice does Joan give?
   ⓐ Blame the manager.   ⓑ Tell the manager.

C. What's your advice? Look at the picture. Tell the worker what to do.

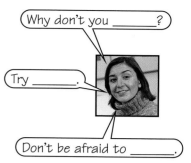

Why don't you _____?

Try _____.

Don't be afraid to _____.

Product warranties and proof-of-purchase cards

Read the warranty and proof-of-purchase card. Answer the questions.

MicroTastic®
Commercial Microwave Oven

Warranty

All warranty service is to be provided by
an authorized MicroTastic® technician.
For service, call 1-800-MTASTIC.

Length of warranty—MicroTastic® will replace or repair:

Full one-year: from date of purchase Any part that fails because of a defect in materials or workmanship. During this one-year period, all parts and labor will be provided free of charge.	**Limited three-year: second through fourth year from date of purchase** The magnetron tube, if it fails because of a defect in materials or workmanship. During this period, purchaser will be responsible for costs of labor.

MicroTastic®

Microwave Oven Models MTMO 3400 and 3405

PROOF OF PURCHASE
(MUST BE SENT IN WITHIN ONE MONTH OF PURCHASE TO ACTIVATE WARRANTY)

Your name _Tina Park_

Your address _131 Stanley Street, Pine Plains, New Jersey 07077_

Where was your MicroTastic® microwave oven purchased?
City Wide Electronics, 2 Central Ave., North Orange, NJ 07079

When was it purchased? _January 1, 2002_

If your MicroTastic® microwave oven needs to be serviced, call the authorized Customer Service Center nearest you. A complete list can be found on the back of this card.

1. Under the terms of the warranty, who has to provide service for the microwave?

   _____

2. What does the purchaser have to do to activate the warranty? _____

   _____

3. Who will pay for the cost of labor if the magnetron tube is replaced in 2003?

   _____

➤ Do it yourself!   A plan-ahead project

What's the warranty for?

How long is it good for?

Pair work. Bring in a product warranty from a product you purchased. If you don't have a warranty, use one on page 154. Compare warranties with a classmate.

B. Listen to the conversation between a customer and an employee at an electronics repair shop. Then listen again and check the malfunctions they talk about.

	crashes	clogs	sticks	jams
1. the paper	☐	☐	☐	☐
2. the fax button	☐	☐	☐	☐
3. the toner hose	☐	☐	☐	☐
4. the computer	☐	☐	☐	☐

C. Choose <u>your</u> response. Fill in the ovals.

1. "Can you believe it? This drill is still under warranty."

   ⓐ That's too bad.　　　　ⓑ That's great.

2. "I'm afraid I'm going to get in trouble."

   ⓐ What a waste of time.　　　　ⓑ Don't worry. It's always good to speak up.

3. "Now it won't work at all."

   ⓐ That's ridiculous.　　　　ⓑ About six months ago.

4. "Uh-oh."

   ⓐ You're kidding.　　　　ⓑ What's the matter?

D. Write the past participle on the line.

1. The fryer was _____ in Taiwan.
   <small>make / made</small>

2. This car was _____ to me by my husband.
   <small>gave / given</small>

3. The best printers are _____ at Martin Electronics.
   <small>sell / sold</small>

4. Was the repair or replace order _____ by the night shift?
   <small>wrote / written</small>

E. Complete each sentence in the passive voice.

1. The fax machines _____ to the shop on May 1.
   <small>bring</small>

2. The sander _____ by the painters last week.
   <small>break</small>

3. The proof of purchase _____ to the company yesterday.
   <small>send</small>

4. The coffee maker _____ by the cafeteria manager.
   <small>repair</small>

F. Write a response to each statement. Use your <u>own</u> words.

1. "I'm really in hot water now!"

    _____

2. "Maybe I should just try to do the work by hand. I don't want anyone to know that I broke the sewing machine."

    _____

3. "I think you should speak up. You won't be blamed."

    _____

G. Read the warranty. If you buy a Spiffy Floor Polisher today, what repairs will the company make under the warranty five years from today? Check the repairs.

Spiffy Floor Polisher PRODUCT WARRANTY

Full one-year
from date of purchase: Any part that fails because of a defect in materials or workmanship.

Lifetime
from date of purchase: The engine, if it fails because of a defect in materials or workmanship. Spiffy will be responsible for all costs.

1. ☐ the handle   2. ☐ the belts   3. ☐ the engine

H. Composition. On a separate sheet of paper, write about the picture on page 40. Say as much as you can.

Now I can
☐ read and understand a product warranty.
☐ admit a possible error.
☐ reassure someone.
☐ express frustration with equipment malfunctions.
☐ troubleshoot a problem.
☐ _____.

Your customers

 Preview

Warm up. What's the problem?

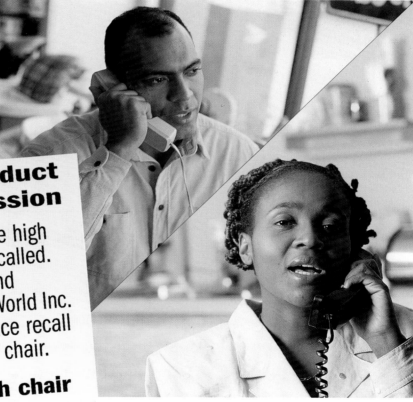

Consumer Product Safety Commission

Defective high chair recalled. CPSC and Infant World Inc. announce recall of high chair.

Infant World high chair

Unit 4 objectives

- Discuss a defective, discontinued, or recalled product.
- Ask for and provide service at a gas station.
- Understand and act on a product safety recall.
- Write and respond to a consumer complaint letter.

Model 1 Discuss a defective item.

A. Listen and read.

A: Hi, Ed. Could you have a look at these faucets?

B: Sure. No problem.

A: The salespeople have been complaining about them.

B: Well, no wonder. They're not up to code.

B. Listen again and repeat.

Poor quality

not up to code
defective
not too good
below standard
no good

Vocabulary

Buyers and sellers

a customer · a dealer · a salesperson

C. Pair work. **Ask your partner to check the quality of these products or the quality of products you make on your job.**

cookies · shower heads · shoes · zippers

A: Hi, _____. Could you have a look at these _____?

B: Sure. No problem.

A: _____ have been complaining about them.

B: Well, no wonder. They're _____.

A. Listen and read.

A: Do you carry Atlas tools?

B: No. We used to carry them, but we don't anymore.

A: Oh, that's a shame. What brand *do* you carry?

B: Hercules. They're just as good and not as expensive.

A: Really?

B: Yes. They're over here. Would you like to have a look?

B. Listen again and repeat.

Locations in a store

over here / over there
in aisle 2
downstairs / upstairs
in the back / in the front

C. Pair work. Discuss brands that the store carries. Use these products or your own ideas.

A: Do you carry _____?

B: No. We used to carry them, but we don't anymore.

A: _____. What brand *do* you carry?

B: _____. They're just as good and not as expensive.

A: _____?

B: _____. They're _____. Would you like to have a look?

➤ Do it yourself!

A. Collaborative activity. Complete the chart about defective products you bought.

I called the dealer and complained.

I exchanged it for something else.

I took it back to the dealer.

Product	Problem	Dealer's name
Primary Paint	wrong color on label	Hardware Mart
1.		
2.		

B. Discussion. What did you do about the defective product?

Model 3 Explain about a discontinued product.

 A. Listen and read.

> **A:** Excuse me. I'm looking for the Speedy shower heads.
>
> **B:** I'm sorry. Those were discontinued. They didn't meet EPA rules.
>
> **A:** That's too bad. They were really great.
>
> **B:** That's what everyone said. But I can show you something else.

🎧 **B.** Listen again and repeat.

🎧 **Good quality**
  great
  fantastic
  effective
  convenient

🎧 **Vocabulary**

Products that have to meet EPA rules and other environmental standards

| toilets | air conditioners | shower heads | pesticides | weed killers |

C. Pair work. **Tell a customer about a discontinued product. Use the vocabulary or other brands and products you know.**

> **A:** Excuse me. I'm looking for the _____.
>
> **B:** I'm sorry. Those were discontinued. They didn't meet EPA rules.
>
> **A:** _____. They were _____.
>
> **B:** _____.

A. Listen and read.

A: Customer Service. How can I help you?

B: I bought a high chair from you, and I heard there's been a recall.

A: Yes, that's true. Please bring it in and we'll give you a replacement.

B: Can I get a credit instead?

A: Absolutely. So long as you have your receipt.

Consumer Product Safety Commission

Defective high chair recalled. CPSC and Infant World Inc. announce recall of high chair.

Infant World high chair

B. Listen again and repeat.

Ways to make good

a replacement
a credit
a refund

Vocabulary

Products for babies and children

a stroller

a crib

a car seat

a high chair

C. Pair work. Discuss a product safety recall. Offer to make good. Use the vocabulary or your <u>own</u> ideas.

A: Customer Service. _____?

B: I bought a _____ from you, and I heard there's been a recall.

A: Yes, that's true. Please bring it in and we'll give you a _____.

B: Can I get a _____ instead?

A: _____.

➤ Do it yourself!

How can I help you?

Pair work. Create a phone conversation about one of the products. Use your <u>own</u> ideas. Say as much as you can.

Qwik Kool

Vesuvius

➤ Practical grammar

Used to

"Do you still carry the Infant World stroller?"

"No. We **used to carry** it, but it was recalled."

Use <u>used to</u> and a verb to talk about something that happened in the past but no longer happens.

Dora Mee **used to live** in China. Now she lives in the United States.

I	
You	
He, She	
We	**used to shop** at Infant World.
You	
They	
Pedro and Pilar	

Questions

Did you **use to** live in Peru?	Yes, I did.
Where did Dora Mee **use to** live?	In China.
Do you carry Atlas tools?	No, but we **used to**.

A. **Read and write about Dora Mee's life in China and the United States.**

in China	in the United States
1. lived in a small town	lives in a large city
2. worked in a hospital	works in a factory
3. ordered supplies	checks quality
4. took a bus to work	drives to work

1. _She used to live in a small town. Now she lives in a large city._

2. _____

3. _____

4. _____

B. **Look at Dora's chart for ideas. Then complete the chart about yourself.**

in my home country	in the United States
1. /	/
2. /	/

C. **Pair work. Ask your partner what he or she used to do and what he or she does now. Then tell the class about your partner.**

Comparisons with <u>as</u> and <u>not</u> <u>as</u>

> Safe-Tee tools are **as good as** Topnotch tools.
> Kick Weed is**n't as effective as** Bug-Dead.
>
> These tools are **not as strong as** they used to be.

D. Write comparisons with <u>as</u> and <u>not as</u>.

1. Lifeline strollers / not safe / Krafty strollers.
   Lifeline strollers are not as safe as Krafty strollers.

2. The hand drill / not fast / the power drill.

3. Small neighborhood stores / not convenient / chain stores.

4. Pesticides / dangerous / weed killers.

Comparative forms: Review

cheaper	more convenient / less convenient	better

E. Write comparisons using comparative forms. Use your <u>own</u> opinions.

1. old cars / new cars
   Old cars are cheaper than new cars.

2. television / radio

3. power tools / hand tools

See page 149 for a list of irregular comparative and superlative forms of adjectives.

➤ Do it yourself!

> The weather in this country is not as hot as the weather in Ecuador.

A. Personalization. Compare the country where you used to live with this country.

	Where I used to live	**This country**
food	spicy	not as spicy
food		
public transportation		
weather		

B. Discussion. Talk to your classmates about your life in the past and your life now.

Authentic practice

🎧 **A.** Read and listen again. Then complete each sentence.

1. The kind of gas the customer asked for was _____.

2. The attendant told him he also needed _____.

3. The brand of oil the service station used to carry is _____.

4. The attendant suggested that the customer check his _____.

🎧 **B.** Listen. Underline **your** response.

1. **YOU** Absolutely.   **YOU** Do you carry Auto-Lube?

2. **YOU** So long as you have the receipt.   **YOU** Yes, please.

3. **YOU** Really?   **YOU** OK, please check the oil.

🎧 **C.** Listen again. Read **your** response out loud.

🎧 **A.** **Listening comprehension. Listen to the announcements. Then listen again and complete each sentence. Fill in the ovals.**

Announcement 1

1. The problem is _____.

   ⓐ a pesticide   ⓑ a container

2. The company is offering _____.

   ⓐ a recall   ⓑ a refund

3. Purchasers should _____.

   ⓐ return the product   ⓑ expose the user to pesticides

Announcement 2

1. The problem is _____.

   ⓐ a four-state recall   ⓑ an infant carrier

2. The company is offering _____.

   ⓐ a refund   ⓑ a repair kit

3. Purchasers should _____.

   ⓐ call a toll-free number   ⓑ return the product

B. **True story. In a group, discuss product safety recalls that you have heard or read about.**

➤ Do it yourself!

A. **Write your <u>own</u> response. Then read your conversation out loud with a partner.**

> Hello, I'm calling about the Jones Gran Turismo infant carrier that was recalled.

YOU _____

> It's model 1311-X. What do I have to do to get the repair kit?

YOU _____

> What a shame that infant carrier was recalled! It was so convenient.

YOU _____

B. **Culture talk. In the country you come from, how do customers deal with defective products? Compare cultures with your classmates.**

Environmental protection laws

🎧 **A.** Read and listen to the letters.

Ask Joan
Culture tips for newcomers

Dear Joan:

I work in a parking garage with some people from the country where I used to live. Sometimes we earn a little extra money running errands and doing favors for our customers, and the boss says that's OK. Well, last week one of my co-workers changed the oil in a customer's car, and he threw the container with the used oil right in the garbage so that it wouldn't make a mess. He closed the container very tight to keep the garage clean.

When the owner of the garage saw the container with the old oil in the garbage, he was very angry. He said he was going to fire my friend! Joan, I don't understand what the big deal is. It was just one container of oil, and he threw it in the garbage, not on the street. The garage owner said it was against the law to throw motor oil in the garbage, that you have to recycle it.

I don't understand. What could one little container of oil do?

Confused in Kentucky

Dear Confused:

In this country we have strict rules about what things you can throw into the garbage and what things you cannot. The U.S. Environmental Protection Agency, the EPA, sets standards, and these rules help us protect the environment. People who violate the rules have to pay large fines. No wonder your boss was so angry!

Used motor oil can get into our water supply and seriously damage it. Some other things that can hurt the environment are batteries, pesticides, weed killers, and other chemicals. Batteries and used motor oil have to be recycled. Your boss can tell you where to find recycling bins. Pesticides, weed killers, and other chemicals have to be disposed of properly. Be sure to read the directions on the containers.

One little container of oil is a small thing, but if everyone threw one container of used oil into the garbage, the problem would be very serious.

Joan

B. Choose an answer to each question. Fill in the ovals.

1. What's the problem?

   ⓐ The oil wasn't disposed of properly.   ⓑ The boss had to pay a fine.

2. What can used motor oil do?

   ⓐ Make a mess in the garbage.   ⓑ Damage the water we drink.

3. What is a <u>fine</u>?

   ⓐ Money you have to pay when you break a rule.   ⓑ The environment.

C. What's your advice? Tell each person what to do.

1. (YOU) _____

2. (YOU) _____

Consumer complaint letters and responses

A. Read the customer complaint letter and the dealer's answer.

Sir or Madam:

I'm writing to complain about the Enviro-Flush toilet I recently purchased at Plumb Good. You used to carry the Vesuvius toilet and it was a very good toilet. It's a shame you don't carry that brand anymore. Your sales staff said that Vesuvius didn't meet EPA guidelines for water conservation and that Enviro-Flush was just as good.

I am <u>very</u> dissatisfied with the Enviro-Flush toilet because I have to flush it four times instead of only once. Please tell me, how is this saving water?

Sincerely,
Peter Plummer

P.S. I have three children. This toilet is <u>not</u> convenient for us.

PLUMB GOOD PLUMBING SUPPLY

1600 South Freemont
Flushing, MI 48433

Dear Mr. Plummer:

I am sorry that you are dissatisfied with the toilet you purchased from us. I'm sure you understand, however, that Plumb Good Plumbing Supply must comply with all EPA standards. Although we cannot, of course, give a refund on a used toilet, we'd be happy to offer you a discount on the next purchase you make at our store.

Sincerely,

Manny Diamante

Manny Diamante

For extra practice, go to page 155.

B. On a separate sheet of paper, write a complaint letter about something you bought.

➤ Do it yourself!

Collaborative activity. Read your partner's letter of complaint. On a separate sheet of paper, write a response letter to your partner. Offer to make good.

🎧 Ways to make good on a complaint

offer a refund
offer an exchange
offer store credit
offer a repair

B. Listen to the conversation between a wife and a husband about a product recall. Read the statements and listen again. Check <u>True</u> or <u>False</u>.

	True	False
1. The product is something to eat.	☐	☐
2. They bought it five minutes ago.	☐	☐
3. They got a recall notice in the mail.	☐	☐
4. The dealer will give them a refund.	☐	☐

C. Choose <u>your</u> response. Fill in the ovals.

1. "People are complaining about these zippers."

   ⓐ It's no wonder. They're defective.   ⓑ What brand do you carry?

2. "The Rapid-Flush toilets were discontinued."

   ⓐ Absolutely.   ⓑ That's a shame.

3. "Can I get a credit?"

   ⓐ Sure. No problem.   ⓑ We don't anymore.

D. Read about Ines Ramirez. Then write about what she used to do and what she does now.

in the past	now
1. lived in Mexico	lives in Denver, Colorado
2. worked in a primary school	works in a high school
3. taught mathematics	teaches Spanish
4. lived in a house	lives in an apartment

1. _She used to live in Mexico. Now she lives in Denver, Colorado._

2. _____

3. _____

4. _____

E. Write comparisons with <u>as</u> and <u>not as</u>. Use your <u>own</u> opinion.

1. Chinese food / spicy / Mexican food.

   _____

2. weather in the fall / warm / weather in the spring.

   _____

3. Buses / convenient / trains.

   _____

F. Write a response to each statement or question. Use your <u>own</u> words.

1. "You used to carry Best Loaf bread. Why don't you carry it anymore?"

   _____

2. "My tires are a little low. Do you have an air pump?"

   _____

3. "I'm down a quart of oil."

   _____

G. Composition. On a separate sheet of paper, write about the picture on page 54. Say as much as you can.

```
Now I can
❑ discuss a defective, discontinued, or
   recalled product.
❑ ask for and provide service at a gas
   station.
❑ understand and act on a product safety
   recall.
❑ write and respond to a consumer
   complaint letter.
❑ _____.
```

Your time

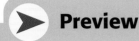

Preview

Warm up. What's "minimum wage"?

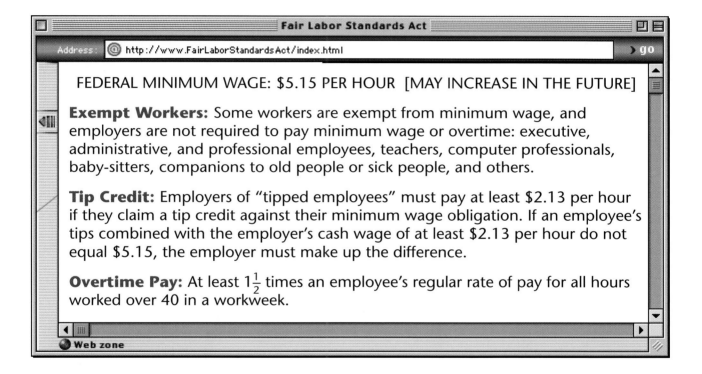

FEDERAL MINIMUM WAGE: $5.15 PER HOUR [MAY INCREASE IN THE FUTURE]

Exempt Workers: Some workers are exempt from minimum wage, and employers are not required to pay minimum wage or overtime: executive, administrative, and professional employees, teachers, computer professionals, baby-sitters, companions to old people or sick people, and others.

Tip Credit: Employers of "tipped employees" must pay at least $2.13 per hour if they claim a tip credit against their minimum wage obligation. If an employee's tips combined with the employer's cash wage of at least $2.13 per hour do not equal $5.15, the employer must make up the difference.

Overtime Pay: At least $1\frac{1}{2}$ times an employee's regular rate of pay for all hours worked over 40 in a workweek.

Unit 5 objectives

- Discuss payment, hours, and overtime pay.
- Reschedule an event.
- Talk about your own time and company time.
- Understand your employer's expectations.
- Understand why it's important to be punctual on the job.

Model 1   Discuss payment options.

🎧 A. Listen and read.

A: I really need to find a job. Tell me, what are you doing these days, Nicole?

B: I'm working as a baby-sitter.

A: A baby-sitter? That's great! Full-time or part-time?

B: Full-time, live-in.

A: How are you paid?

B: By the hour, plus room and board.

🎧 B. Listen again and repeat.

🎧 Vocabulary

Occupations and payment options

a gardener:
paid by the hour

a messenger:
paid by the job

a companion:
paid by the week

a waiter / waitress:
paid by the hour, plus tips

a mover:
paid by the hour, plus tips

a taxi driver:
paid by the trip, plus tips

C. Pair work. Discuss jobs and payment options. Use the vocabulary or your <u>own</u> jobs.

A: I really need to find a job. Tell me, what are you doing these days, _____?

B: I'm working as _____.

A: _____. Full-time or part-time?

B: _____.

A: How are you paid?

B: By the _____.

A. Listen and read.

A: What are the hours?

B: Eight to five and an hour for lunch.

A: And could you please tell me what the pay is?

B: We pay minimum wage, time and a half for overtime, and double time on Sundays and holidays.

A: Could you repeat that, please? I'd like to make a note of it.

B. Listen again and repeat.

Vocabulary

Wages and hours

minimum wage: $5.15 per hour   time and a half: $7.73   double time: $10.30

C. Pair work. Talk about hours and overtime pay. Use the ads or your <u>own</u> hours and pay.

A: What are the hours?

B: _____.

A: And could you please tell me what the pay is?

B: We pay _____ and _____.

A: _____?

> **PARKING ATTENDANT**
> Minimum wage $5.15/hr. + tips
> Overtime pay: time and a half
> Shifts: first: 7am to 3pm with
>   one-hour break for lunch.
> second: 3pm to 11pm with
>   one-hour break for dinner.

> • BEAUTICIAN'S ASSISTANT •
> Pt.-time Immediate
> Responsibilities: wash clients'
> hair.   Salary: $4.80/hr.
> plus tips. Hours: Tuesdays
> & Wednesdays 11:00 a.m. to
> 4:00 p.m. Experienced only.

➤ Do it yourself!

Collaborative activity. Make a list of the occupations of the students in the class. Write the list on the chalkboard.

Occupations	How paid?
live-in home health aide	by the month + room and board

Practical conversations

🎧 **A. Listen and read.**

A: I'm sorry, but I have to reschedule our meeting. I have to go to the dentist.

B: No problem. When do you want to reschedule?

A: How's tomorrow, after lunch?

B: Actually, that won't work. How about tomorrow morning at 10?

A: Yeah. That's good for me.

🎧 **B. Listen again and repeat.**

🎧 **Time expressions**

after
before
during

🎧 **Vocabulary**

Reasons to reschedule events

I have a problem at home.

I have a family problem.

I'm not feeling well.

I have to run an errand.

C. Pair work. Reschedule an event from the box. Give your <u>own</u> reason.

lunch	appointment	meeting	dinner

A: I'm sorry, but I have to reschedule our _____. I _____.

B: _____. When do you want to reschedule?

A: How's _____?

B: Actually, that won't work. How about _____?

A: _____.

A. Listen and read.

A: I need to speak to my friend. Is that a problem?

B: Is it an emergency?

A: No, not really.

B: Well, unless it's an emergency, we expect you to do that on your own time. Why don't you do that at lunch time?

B. Listen again and repeat.

Personal time

on your own time
at break time
at lunch time
after closing time

Vocabulary

Personal activities

make a phone call

speak to Human Resources

go to the restroom

C. Pair work. Ask for permission. Use the vocabulary or your <u>own</u> activities.

A: I need to _____. Is that a problem?

B: Is it an emergency?

A: _____.

B: Well, unless it's an emergency, we expect you to do that on your own time. Why don't you do that _____?

➤ Do it yourself!

What's your opinion? What's OK to do on company time? What should you do on your own time? Discuss with a partner or a group.

1. read the newspaper
2. get a cup of coffee
3. go to the restroom
4. go to the dentist
5. use the Internet
6. other: _____

➤ Practical grammar

Verbs followed by infinitives

Use infinitives after the following verbs: <u>be sure</u>, <u>decide</u>, <u>forget</u>, <u>need</u>, <u>plan</u>, <u>remember</u>, <u>want</u>.

> Lynn **decided to look for** a new job.
>
> They **forgot to reschedule** the meeting.
>
> **Remember to dispose of** pesticides properly.

A. Complete the paragraph with verbs and infinitives.

Pennsylvania Pipe Company

Policies and Procedures

Time off with pay

When you _____ a personal day, _____
    <u>1. decide / take</u>   <u>2. be sure / ask</u>

your manager in advance. Let him or her know that you _____
                                                          <u>3. need / be</u>

out of the office. Also, _____ your manager when you
                            <u>4. not forget / tell</u>

_____ to work.
    <u>5. plan / return</u>

                                                        Pennsylvania Pipe

---

See page 149 for a list of verbs followed by infinitives.

Verbs followed by objects and infinitives

Use an object and an infinitive after <u>ask</u>, <u>tell</u>, <u>expect</u>, <u>invite</u>, <u>would like</u>, <u>warn</u>, <u>help</u>, <u>want</u>, and <u>remind</u> when you talk about another person.

      object   infinitive   object infinitive

Please **ask Martin** not **to leave**.   We **expect her to call**.

B. Write your **own** sentences with these subjects, verbs, objects, and infinitive phrases.

Subjects	Verbs	Objects	Infinitive phrases
I	expect	us	to call
You	want	her	to tell me
She	invite	him	to reschedule lunch
He	remind	you	not to park in the small lot
Ivan	warn	us	to pay us by the hour
Ms. Smith	ask	them	to give him a tip
We	tell	Glenda	to get time and a half
They	would like	Alan	to make a note of that

1. *He asked Glenda to reschedule lunch.*
2. _____
3. _____
4. _____
5. _____
6. _____

See page 150 for a list of list of verbs followed by objects and infinitives.

➤ Do it yourself!

A. **Personalization. What do people expect you to do? Write about expectations people have of you at work, at home, and at school.**

at work	
	My boss expects me to come to work on time.
at work	
	_____
at home	
	_____
at school	
	_____

B. **Discussion. Compare your answers with a partner or a group.**

🎧 **A.** **Read and listen again. Then choose the word or phrase that has the same meaning.**

1. Sometimes it's not easy to find a <u>backup</u> on short notice.

    ⓐ a replacement   ⓑ a porter

2. Sometimes it's not easy to find a backup <u>on short notice</u>.

    ⓐ with a lot of time   ⓑ with only a little time

3. I have to <u>postpone</u> our lunch meeting again.

    ⓐ reschedule for an earlier time   ⓑ reschedule for a later time

🎧 **B.** **Listen. Underline <u>your</u> response.**

1. **YOU** Thanks so much.   **YOU** From porter to bell captain.

2. **YOU** Absolutely.   **YOU** That's very dangerous.

3. **YOU** That's OK. What's up?   **YOU** On the contrary.

🎧 **C.** **Listen again. Read <u>your</u> response out loud.**

Clarifying employers' instructions

🎧 **A. Listening comprehension. Listen to the conversation between an employer and a baby-sitter. Listen again and check what Mr. Gomez expects the baby-sitter to do.**

Mr. Gomez expects the baby-sitter

1. ☐ to order pizza.
2. ☐ to give the delivery man a tip.
3. ☐ to remind Lisa to do her homework.
4. ☐ to help Lisa with her homework.
5. ☐ to watch TV with Lisa.
6. ☐ to remind Jaime to do his homework.
7. ☐ to call him if Jaime has a cold.

B. True story. What are your responsibilities at home or at work? What do other people expect you to do? Tell your partner or your group.

➤ Do it yourself!

A. Write your own response. Then read your conversation out loud with a partner.

You said you were looking for some part-time work. I have something for you.

YOU _____

Charlie called in sick. Do you think you could fill in for him? We could pay you overtime . . . time and a half.

YOU _____

Any questions?

YOU _____

B. Culture talk. In the country you come from, do you have to tell an employer in advance that you can't come to work? Compare cultures with your classmates.

Punctuality and consideration of others

🎧 **A.** Read and listen to the letters.

Ask Joan
Culture tips for newcomers

Dear Joan:
I wrote you a few months ago to ask when to arrive at a dinner party that was scheduled for 6:00, and you told me to arrive by about 6:15. Joan, I trusted your advice, and now I'm in big trouble at work!

I had my performance review yesterday, and my supervisor said I was a great worker, but that I can't get a raise until I am more punctual. I was afraid to ask him to explain, but I don't understand. I always follow your advice, and when my lunch or my break is over, I always go right back to work in fifteen or twenty minutes. Am I doing something wrong?

Nadia, even more nervous

Dear Nadia:
At work it's very important to be punctual. No employer will tolerate lateness because it causes problems for the whole team. If you are not on time at your job, someone else will have to do your work.

Your supervisor expects you to come in on time, return from breaks and lunch on time, and do personal business on your own time, not company time. If for some reason you have an emergency or you can't be on time, be sure to give your boss as much advance warning as possible, so he or she can plan to fill in with someone who can do your job temporarily.

If you follow these rules and keep being a good worker, I'm sure you'll get a raise in no time!

Joan

B. Choose an answer to each question. Fill in the ovals.

1. What's the problem?

   ⓐ Nadia isn't punctual.   ⓑ Nadia does personal business on company time.

2. Nadia's lunch hour ends at 1:10. When does her boss expect her to be at her desk?

   ⓐ 1:10   ⓑ 1:30

3. What should Nadia do if she has an emergency and can't be on time for work?

   ⓐ call her boss first   ⓑ come in late and then explain the problem

C. What's your advice? Tell each co-worker what to do.

My son has a fever, and the school nurse asked me to come get him. But my shift is just starting. What should I do?

I need to run across the street to pick up a couple of videos. It'll only take 15 minutes. What do you think?

1. (YOU) _____   2. (YOU) _____

Overtime pay

A. Read about the minimum wage taken from the Fair Labor Standards Act.

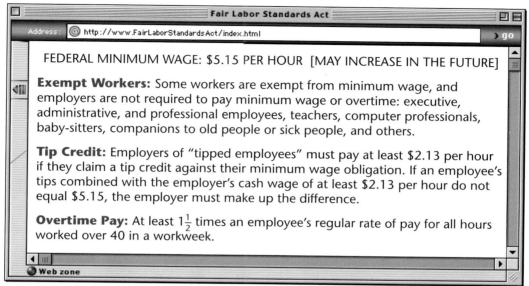

For extra practice, go to page 156.

B. Read these want ads.

Help Wanted

NURSE—LPN or RN
Medicaid # needed. $24/hr.
Private home. 914 555 8700

Now Hiring
OFFICE MGMT/SECRETARY
FT position. Casual environ-
ment. Will train right person.
Must be responsible. 621-
9555

Help Wanted

WAITRESS/WAITER
PT/FT/WEEKENDS
$4.50 / + tips; FT (40 hrs per wk)
SHORT-ORDER COOK
Also wanted
Minimum wage. Time + 1/2
for OT, 2x on Sundays and
Holidays. Apply in person at
Cindy's Diner, 28 Chambers
St.

Help Wanted

** Sales Reps **
Earn $12.50 to $50 per hour.
Must have 3 yrs experience.
Evenings: 5–9:30 &
Saturdays: 10–2 p.m.
Call 201 555 4360

SECRETARY
Full-time; phones, MS Word,
Accts Receivable & Payable
experience. Please call:

C. Read about the people who got the jobs and how much they earned.
Then check **T** (true), **F** (false), or **?** (not enough information to answer).

	T	F	?
1. Raul Santini got the nurse's job. Last week he worked 56 hours. He earned $1536.	☐	☐	☐
2. Golda Moskowitz got the short-order cook's job. She worked 40 hours from Monday to Friday and 6 hours on Saturday and on Sunday. She earned $314.18.	☐	☐	☐
3. Ken Park got the sales rep's job. He worked 35 hours last week. He earned $1050.	☐	☐	☐

➤ Do it yourself!   A plan-ahead project

A. Bring in want ads from your local newspaper. Find a job that pays by the hour, one that pays by the week, and one other kind.

B. Discussion. Compare ads with your classmates.

Review

A. Pair work or group work.

- Where are the people?
- What are their problems?

Ask and answer questions.

Create conversations.

Tell a story.

Say as much as you can.

B. **Listen to the conversation about wages and hours. Read the questions and listen again. Answer the questions. Fill in the ovals.**

1. Which job is part-time?

   (a) the cafeteria manager   (b) the mailroom manager

2. What's the weekly pay for the mailroom manager?

   (a) $600.00   (b) $340.00

3. Which is more important to the applicant?

   (a) flexibility   (b) money

C. **Complete each sentence. Fill in the ovals.**

1. A waiter or a waitress gets a salary plus _____.

   (a) tips   (b) minimum wage

2. The hours are _____ with a one-hour break for lunch.

   (a) 9 to 5   (b) $4.80

3. Don't do that on _____.

   (a) Human Resources   (b) company time

4. I have to run _____.

   (a) an errand   (b) an emergency

D. **Complete each sentence with an object and an infinitive. Use your _own_ ideas.**

1. She invited _her mother to go shopping._____

2. Peter reminded _____

3. They always ask _____

4. The baby-sitter warned _____

5. We would like _____

6. His children expect _____

E. **Read each sentence. Write your _own_ response.**

1. "How do you get paid on your new job?"

   (YOU) _____

2. "What are you doing these days?"

   (YOU) _____

3. "I'm sorry, but I'm going to have to reschedule."

   (YOU) _____

F. Write your expectations of your boss, your teacher, and one other person.
Use your <u>own</u> ideas.

1. my boss *I expect my boss to give me a raise this year.*

2. my boss _____

3. my teacher _____

4. _____

G. Read the ads.

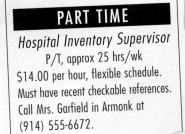

Now read about each person. Choose a job for each one. Fill in the ovals.

1. Lucinda Apu is a night student at a technical college. She needs a part-time job.
Which job is better for her?

   (a) hospital inventory supervisor   (b) teacher's aide

2. Luis Leon needs to earn $350 per week. He has a child at home and only has a
baby-sitter two days a week. Which job is better for him?

   (a) hospital inventory supervisor   (b) teacher's aide

H. Composition. On a separate sheet of paper, write about the picture on page 68.
Say as much as you can.

> **Now I can**
> ❏ discuss payment, hours, and overtime pay.
> ❏ reschedule an event.
> ❏ talk about my own time and company time.
> ❏ understand my employer's expectations.
> ❏ understand why it's important to be
>   punctual on the job.
> ❏ _____ .

Your supplies and resources

Preview

Warm up. Which is the best buy?

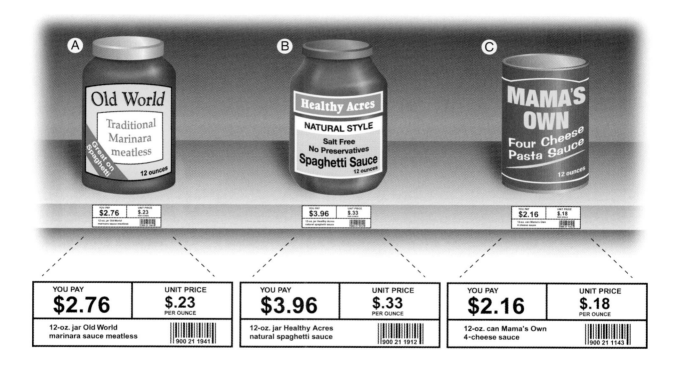

A	
YOU PAY **$2.76**	UNIT PRICE **$.23** PER OUNCE
12-oz. jar Old World marinara sauce meatless	‖‖‖‖ 900 21 1941 ‖‖‖

B	
YOU PAY **$3.96**	UNIT PRICE **$.33** PER OUNCE
12-oz. jar Healthy Acres natural spaghetti sauce	‖‖‖‖ 900 21 1912 ‖‖‖

C	
YOU PAY **$2.16**	UNIT PRICE **$.18** PER OUNCE
12-oz. can Mama's Own 4-cheese sauce	‖‖‖‖ 900 21 1143 ‖‖‖

Unit 6 objectives

- Determine the best buy.
- Talk about bargains.
- Order supplies online and by phone.
- Understand and use unit pricing.

Model 1 Talk about bargains.

🎧 **A.** **Listen and read.**

> **A:** What a bargain! Three cans of tuna for a dollar!
>
> **B:** Really? They're usually 89 cents each. That must be a mistake.
>
> **A:** No. Look at the coupon. It's a seven-ounce can.
>
> **B:** Wow, that *is* a bargain.
>
> **A:** You can say *that* again!

🎧 **B.** **Listen again and repeat.**

🎧 **Vocabulary**

How food is sold

| a can | a loaf | a box | a package | a container |

C. Pair work. **Describe a bargain. Use the coupons or your <u>own</u> ideas.**

Bargains: This week only.   All are FOODWAY BRAND.

12-oz. pkg
Cheddar cheese
3 for $1.59
Reg. $.99 ea.

32-oz. bottle
Apple juice
2 for $1.29
Reg. $.89 ea.

1-gal. cont.
Milk
2 for $3.29
Reg. $2.49 ea.

1-pint jar
Tomato sauce
3 for $3.00
Reg. $1.59 ea.

10-lb. bag
Potatoes
2 for $2.99
Reg. $2.99 ea.

> **A:** What a bargain! _____ for _____!
>
> **B:** Really? _____ usually _____. That must be a mistake.
>
> **A:** No. Look at the coupon. It's a _____.
>
> **B:** Wow, that *is* a bargain.
>
> **A:** You can say *that* again!

A. Listen and read.

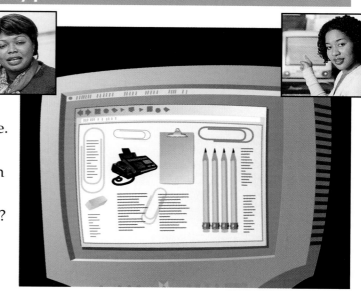

> **A:** I need to go shopping for office supplies.
> **B:** Can I make a suggestion? Order them by phone or online.
> **A:** How?
> **B:** Call 1-800-NOTEPAD or log on to paperclips.com.
> **A:** Hey, why didn't *I* think of that?

B. Listen again and repeat.

Vocabulary

Things to order by phone or online

| clothes | auto parts | uniforms | safety equipment |

C. Pair work. **Make suggestions. Use the vocabulary and the information in the box.**

1-800-CLOTHES	1-800-ANYTHING	your_closets.com
1-800-555-CARPART	auto_parts.com	safety_first.com

> **A:** I need to go shopping for _____.
> **B:** Can I make a suggestion? Order _____ by phone or online.
> **A:** _____?
> **B:** Call _____ or log on to _____.
> **A:** Hey, why didn't *I* think of that?

➤ Do it yourself!

A. **What do you buy at a store, by phone, or online? Complete the chart.**

At a store	By telephone	Online
cleaning supplies		

B. Discussion. **Where do you get the best bargains? Compare opinions with your classmates.**

Conclusions with must

A gallon of ice cream for $2.00? That **must be** a mistake. It usually costs five something.

You're right. It **must not be** the gallon container.

Use must and must not to guess a reason for something you are almost sure of.

I see Linda on the bus every day at 7:30. She **must work** the early shift.

A. Match each statement with a conclusion. Write the letter on the line.

1. Arlene bought 24 cans of cleanser. _____
2. She always buys shoes at Harry's. _____
3. My boss was going to call, but he didn't. _____
4. Roger never goes to the store for parts. _____
5. The waiters only earn $3.50 per hour. _____

a. He must not have my number.
b. It must be cheaper by the case.
c. They must have great bargains.
d. They must get a lot in tips.
e. He must shop by phone or online.

B. Complete each conclusion. Use must and the verb.

1. What a great price for that soup! It _____ on sale.

be

2. Pilar always orders online. She _____ her own computer.

have

3. Ilhan buys only Golden Fields bread. He _____ that brand.

like

4. The nurses always shop there. They _____ the largest selection.

offer

5. That package is cheaper than this one. This _____ the best buy.

not be

Exclamations with What

What beautiful cheese!

And **what** great prices!

What a nice tie!

$6⁹⁹ $5⁹⁹ $4⁹⁹

C. Complete each exclamation with __What__.

1. _____ great car! It must be really expensive.

2. Look at this screen! _____ fabulous prices! Let's order from them.

3. _____ gigantic loaf of bread! We'll never finish it.

Look, dear. I won two movie tickets. What luck!

4. Great! We'll go tonight. _____ fun!

5. I can't believe this. _____ low salaries!

6. This place is pretty expensive. But _____ delicious food!

➤ Do it yourself!

Say something about each box. Then guess what's in it.

What a big box from Notepad!

NOTEPAD OFFICE SUPPLIES

Hey, it must be the new printer!

A. Read and listen again. Then check <u>True</u>, <u>False</u>, or <u>Maybe</u>.

	True	False	Maybe
1. The boy wants Star cheese.	☐	☐	☐
2. The clerk understands unit pricing.	☐	☐	☐
3. The father thinks Star cheese tastes better than Wow Cow.	☐	☐	☐
4. The big package of Wow Cow costs less per pound than the small package.	☐	☐	☐

B. Listen. Underline <u>your</u> response.

1. (YOU) Right! What a difference! (YOU) What's in it?

2. (YOU) I won't buy it. (YOU) You can say *that* again.

3. (YOU) Not always. (YOU) That's a shame.

C. Listen again. Read <u>your</u> response out loud.

🎧 **A.** Listening comprehension. **Listen to the conversation about ordering supplies online.**

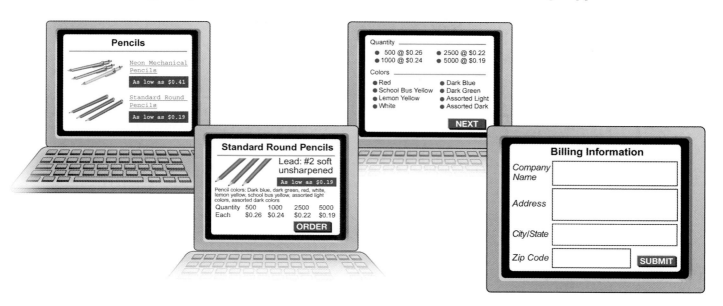

🎧 **B.** Listen again. **Circle the item or items on each screen that Gloria clicks on.**

C. Answer the questions about Gloria's order.

1. What did she order? _____

2. How many? What color? _____

➤ Do it yourself!

A. Write your <u>own</u> response. **Then read your conversation out loud with a partner.**

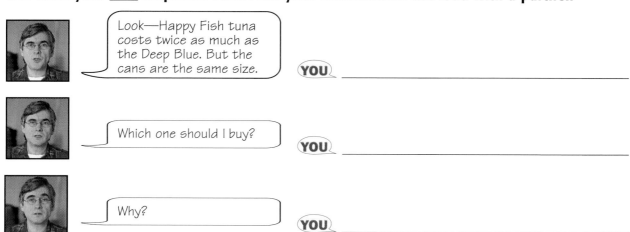

B. Culture talk. **In the country you come from, what is the children's role in choosing foods for the family? Compare cultures with your classmates.**

Authentic practice

Unit pricing

A. Read about unit pricing from a consumer information Web site.

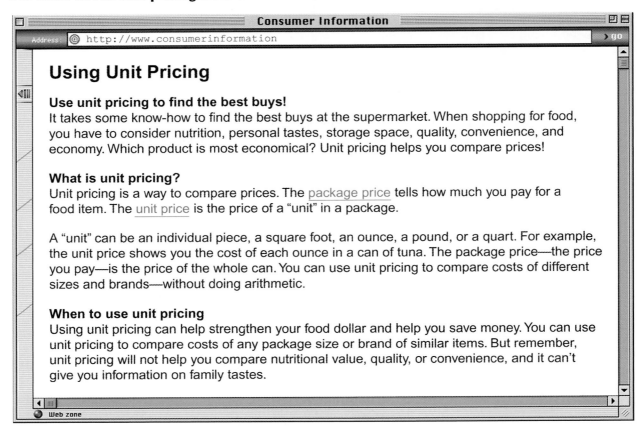

Consumer Information

Address: @ http://www.consumerinformation

Using Unit Pricing

Use unit pricing to find the best buys!
It takes some know-how to find the best buys at the supermarket. When shopping for food, you have to consider nutrition, personal tastes, storage space, quality, convenience, and economy. Which product is most economical? Unit pricing helps you compare prices!

What is unit pricing?
Unit pricing is a way to compare prices. The package price tells how much you pay for a food item. The unit price is the price of a "unit" in a package.

A "unit" can be an individual piece, a square foot, an ounce, a pound, or a quart. For example, the unit price shows you the cost of each ounce in a can of tuna. The package price—the price you pay—is the price of the whole can. You can use unit pricing to compare costs of different sizes and brands—without doing arithmetic.

When to use unit pricing
Using unit pricing can help strengthen your food dollar and help you save money. You can use unit pricing to compare costs of any package size or brand of similar items. But remember, unit pricing will not help you compare nutritional value, quality, or convenience, and it can't give you information on family tastes.

Web zone

B. Read the statements about unit pricing. Then check <u>True</u> or <u>False</u>.

	True	False
1. Unit pricing tells you which product to buy.	☐	☐
2. Unit pricing can help you compare prices of similar foods in different-size packages.	☐	☐
3. The unit price is the price of the package.	☐	☐
4. To get the unit price of a product, you have to do arithmetic.	☐	☐
5. Unit pricing gives you information about how convenient a product is or whether you will like it.	☐	☐

C. Discussion. Look at the unit price labels for tomato sauce. Compare the products. Then decide which sauce to buy. Explain your answer to a partner or a group.

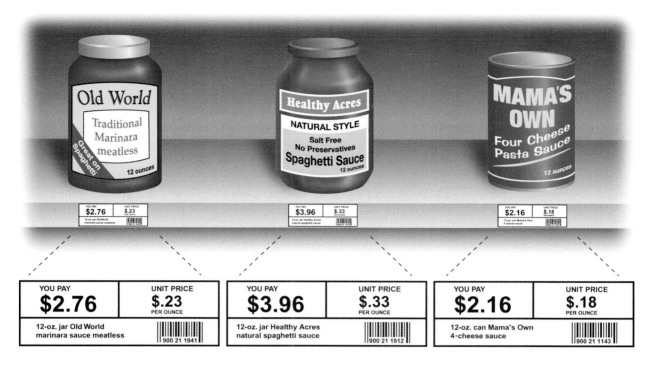

YOU PAY	UNIT PRICE
$2.76	**$.23** PER OUNCE
12-oz. jar Old World marinara sauce meatless	900 21 1941

YOU PAY	UNIT PRICE
$3.96	**$.33** PER OUNCE
12-oz. jar Healthy Acres natural spaghetti sauce	900 21 1912

YOU PAY	UNIT PRICE
$2.16	**$.18** PER OUNCE
12-oz. can Mama's Own 4-cheese sauce	900 21 1143

➤ Do it yourself! A plan-ahead project

A. Go to the store. Choose one example of each product. Look at the package price and the unit price on the shelf. Write them on the chart.

Product	Brand and package price	Unit price from shelf
Chicken soup	*Grandma's brand 89¢*	*$.09 per fluid ounce*
Chicken soup		
Laundry detergent		
Cooking oil		
Rice		

B. Discussion. Compare information with the class.

Authentic practice

A. Read about how to use unit pricing from the Web site.

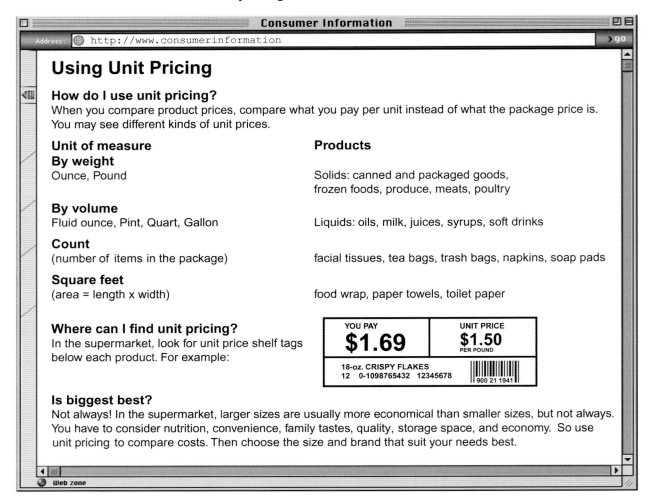

Consumer Information

Address: @ http://www.consumerinformation

Using Unit Pricing

How do I use unit pricing?
When you compare product prices, compare what you pay per unit instead of what the package price is. You may see different kinds of unit prices.

Unit of measure	Products
By weight Ounce, Pound	Solids: canned and packaged goods, frozen foods, produce, meats, poultry
By volume Fluid ounce, Pint, Quart, Gallon	Liquids: oils, milk, juices, syrups, soft drinks
Count (number of items in the package)	facial tissues, tea bags, trash bags, napkins, soap pads
Square feet (area = length x width)	food wrap, paper towels, toilet paper

Where can I find unit pricing?
In the supermarket, look for unit price shelf tags below each product. For example:

YOU PAY	UNIT PRICE
$1.69	**$1.50** PER POUND
18-oz. CRISPY FLAKES 12 0-1098765432 12345678	900 21 1941

Is biggest best?
Not always! In the supermarket, larger sizes are usually more economical than smaller sizes, but not always. You have to consider nutrition, convenience, family tastes, quality, storage space, and economy. So use unit pricing to compare costs. Then choose the size and brand that suit your needs best.

Web zone

B. Collaborative activity. Complete the chart with a group. For each unit of measure, list the products that group members buy. Then compare charts with other groups.

Unit of measure	Products
Ounce	
Pound	
Fluid ounce	
Pint	

Unit of measure	Products
Quart	
Gallon	
Count	
Square feet	

A. Look at the order form for office supplies.

| R | Robinson Office Products | | | | | Order form |

Submitted by _____   Company name _____

Billing address _____

Item	QTY	UM	Description	Price	Total
BINDERS					
B3401	_	EA	Binder vinyl 1" black	$2.39	_____
B3402	_	EA	Binder vinyl 2" black	$3.39	_____
B3403	_	EA	Binder vinyl 1" white	$2.39	_____
B3404	_	EA	Binder vinyl 2" white	$3.39	_____
CLIPS					
C3401	_	BX	Clips jumbo smooth	$2.29	_____
C3402	_	BX	Clips mini smooth	$1.19	_____
PENS					
P3401	_	DZ	Fine markers blue	$11.99	_____
P3402	_	DZ	Ballpoint medium black	$10.99	_____

B. Discussion. What do the abbreviations mean? Explain to a partner or a group.

1. QTY _____

2. UM _____

3. EA _____

4. BX _____

5. DZ _____

C. Now fill out the order form. Order supplies for ABC Oil Company at 2200 Main Street in Dallas, Texas 75219. Choose your supplies and use your <u>own</u> name.

For extra practice, go to page 157.

➤ Do it yourself!

Discussion. How do you buy supplies? First make notes about your ideas on the chart. Then discuss the advantages and disadvantages of each way.

Going to the store	
advantage *You can see the product.*	disadvantage *It takes a lot of time.*
advantage	disadvantage
Ordering by mail from a catalogue	
advantage	disadvantage
Shopping online	
advantage	disadvantage

B. Listen to the conversation about ordering supplies. Read the statements and listen again. Check <u>True</u> or <u>False</u>.

	True	False
1. The men repair car air conditioners.	☐	☐
2. They can't fix the problem because they don't have enough parts.	☐	☐
3. They order hoses online.	☐	☐
4. The company is going to send the parts by regular mail.	☐	☐
5. The man orders more parts because delivery is a bargain.	☐	☐

C. Match the abbreviation with the word. Write the letter on the line.

1. ____ DZ
2. ____ EA
3. ____ UM
4. ____ QTY

a. quantity
b. one dozen (12)
c. unit of measure
d. each

D. Write the name of each kind of package.

1. _____ 2. _____ 3. _____ 4. _____

E. Write a response to each statement.

1. "I have no time to go to the store."

_____

2. "What a bargain!"

_____

F. Write a conclusion with <u>must</u>.

1. Jose Antonio always buys milk in two-gallon containers.

_____

2. Look at this huge box. What's in it?

_____

3. Claire wants to be a teacher.

_____

G. Complete each exclamation with <u>What</u>.

1. _____ can of soup! How much does it cost?
   big

2. _____ food. Let's eat here again.
   wonderful

H. Choose the correct answer to each question about unit pricing. Fill in the ovals.

1. What does unit pricing tell you?
   - ⓐ Which product to buy.
   - ⓑ The cost of each unit of a product.

2. What is the advantage of unit pricing?
   - ⓐ It helps you compare prices of products in different-size containers.
   - ⓑ It tells you the package price.

3. What CANNOT be learned from a unit price?
   - ⓐ The price of a unit of the product.
   - ⓑ The best product.

I. Which peaches have the lower unit price? Fill in the oval.

ⓐ Orchard's Pride   ⓑ Tasty Fruit

YOU PAY **$2.49**	UNIT PRICE **$.21** per fluid ounce
12-oz. can Orchard's Pride cling peaches in heavy syrup	900 42 0818

YOU PAY **$2.99**	UNIT PRICE **$.18** per fluid ounce
17-oz. can Tasty Fruit cling peaches in heavy syrup	900 21 1912

J. Composition. On a separate sheet of paper, write about the picture on page 82. Say as much as you can.

Now I can
- ❑ determine the best buy.
- ❑ talk about bargains.
- ❑ order supplies online and by phone.
- ❑ understand and use unit pricing.
- ❑ _____.

Your relationships

 Preview

Warm up. What's the problem?

Unit 7 objectives

- Ask about and understand rules and laws.
- Ask someone to be more considerate.
- Apologize for inconsiderate behavior.
- Understand personal responsibility to know and obey rules and laws.
- Make small talk.
- Congratulate someone on good news.
- Express sympathy and offer to help.

Model 1   Ask someone to be more considerate. Apologize for your behavior.

🎧 **A. Listen and read.**

A: Excuse me. Would it be possible for you to turn down the music? It's after 11:00.

B: Oh, I'm sorry. I didn't realize that.

A: Thanks. I appreciate it.

B: You're welcome.

🎧 **B. Listen again and repeat.**

🎧 Vocabulary

Difficult requests

to turn down the music

to park somewhere else

to get off the phone

to put out the cigarette

to move the truck

to close the window

C. Pair work. Ask someone to do something. Use the vocabulary and the reasons in the box. Or use your own reasons.

I can't get into my driveway.	It's very cold in here.
It's too loud to work.	I'm having trouble sleeping.
That's my parking space.	I'm allergic to smoke.
I'm waiting for an important call.	It's really late.

A: Excuse me. Would it be possible for you to _____? _____.

B: Oh, I'm sorry. I didn't realize that.

A: _____.

B: _____.

Model 2 Ask about rules and laws. Admit that you're not sure.

A. Listen and read.

A: Excuse me. Is it legal to park here?
B: Well, to tell you the truth, I'm not sure. Why don't you ask him?

A: Excuse me. Is it OK to park here?
C: As far as I know, it is.

B. Listen again and repeat.

To say you're not sure
I'm not sure.
I don't know.
I have no idea.
I'm not positive.

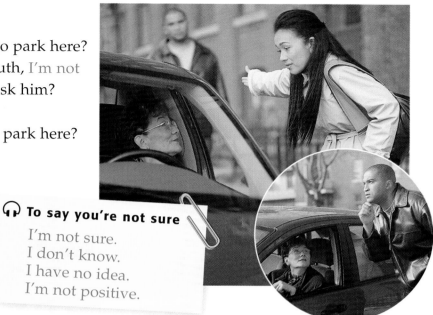

Vocabulary

Things that might be against the rules or the law

to put the trash cans here   to let a dog off the leash   to make a right turn on red

C. Group work. Ask two people about rules or the law. Use the vocabulary or your own question about rules or the law.

A: _____. Is it legal to _____?
B: Well, to tell you the truth, _____. Why don't you ask _____?

A: _____. Is it OK for me to _____?
C: As far as I know, it is.

➤ Do it yourself!

Collaborative activity. **Make a list of things you were surprised to learn are illegal here. Then discuss your list with other groups.**

It's illegal here to let a dog off the leash.

_____

_____

_____

Practical conversations

Model 3 Make small talk. Talk about good news.

A. Listen and read.

> **A:** Hey, Steve. How are things?
> **B:** Pretty good. What about you?
> **A:** Great, actually. I just got engaged.
> **B:** Congratulations. I'm really happy to hear that.

B. Listen again and repeat.

To start a conversation

How are things?	How are you?
How's it going?	What's up?
How're you doing?	What's new?

Vocabulary

Happy occasions

get engaged   get married   have a baby   have a grandchild   get a promotion

C. Pair work. Make small talk about a happy event in your life or the life of a relative. Use the vocabulary or your <u>own</u> happy event.

> **A:** Hey, _____. _____?
> **B:** _____. What about you?
> **A:** Great, actually. _____.
> **B:** Congratulations. I'm really happy to hear that.

A. Listen and read.

A: You look upset. Is there anything wrong?

B: Well, actually, my sister and my brother-in-law are getting a divorce.

A: Oh, I'm so sorry to hear that. Is there anything I can do?

B: Not really. But thanks for offering. I appreciate it.

B. Listen again and repeat.

Unhappy feelings

upset	sad
down	depressed

Vocabulary

Unhappy occasions

have a death in the family

get separated

get a divorce

get laid off *or* lose a job

C. Pair work. Talk about an unhappy event. Offer sympathy and help.

A: You look _____. Is there anything wrong?

B: Well, actually, _____.

A: Oh, I'm so sorry to hear that. Is there anything I can do?

B: _____. But thanks for offering. I appreciate it.

➤ Do it yourself!

Pair work. Create a conversation for the people. Say as much as you can.

Practical grammar

It's wrong to throw trash on the ground.

Oh, I'm sorry.

Express judgments with It is + an adjective and an infinitive. Here are some adjectives of judgment:

polite	right	inconvenient
impolite	great	possible
rude	hard	impossible
important	easy	good
wrong	convenient	bad

A. Complete each sentence with a judgment.

1. ___It's___ bad _____to be_____ rude to your neighbors.
                        be

2. _____ important _____ all the rules.
                                learn

3. _____ rude _____ music too loud.
                      play

4. _____ wrong _____ trash on the street.
                       put

5. _____ very convenient _____ in your own driveway.
                                    park

6. _____ not difficult _____ a promotion here.
                               get

B. Write a question from the cues. Then ask your partner each question. Your partner answers in his or her own words.

1. legal / park in a bus stop?

   A: _Is it legal to park in a bus stop?_____

   B: _____

2. possible / get a divorce in all countries?

   A: _____

   B: _____

3. easy / ask your neighbor to move his or her car?

   A: _____

   B: _____

90   Unit 7

4. wrong / let your dog off the leash?

A: _____

B: _____

5. good / get married when you're very young?

A: _____

B: _____

C. Rewrite each sentence. Express the ideas in another way.

1. Parking here is illegal. _It's illegal to park here._ _____

2. Playing music late at night is rude. _____

_____

3. Getting a divorce is terrible. _____

_____

4. Is driving a truck hard? _____

_____

5. Was calling my supervisor at home impolite? _____

_____

➤ Do it yourself!

A. Personalization. **Compare customs and laws in your country and in this country.**

Custom	_In my country, it's OK to ask a co-worker about salary or religion. In this country, those questions are impolite._
Law	_In my country, it's legal to cross the street wherever you want. Here, jaywalking is against the law._
Custom	_____
	_____
Law	_____
	_____
	_____

B. Discussion. **Compare customs and laws with your classmates. How are they different?**

For extra practice, go to page 158.

Authentic practice

🎧 **A. Read and listen again. Choose the word or phrase closer in meaning to the underlined word or phrase. Fill in the ovals.**

1. "Listen to that <u>racket</u>."

    ⓐ work   ⓑ noise

2. "Why don't you just ask them <u>to keep it down</u>?"

    ⓐ to talk less loudly   ⓑ to make noise

3. "I'm sure they don't even realize <u>they're bothering you</u>."

    ⓐ they're helping you   ⓑ they're making it difficult for you

4. "Could I ask you two <u>a big favor</u>?"

    ⓐ to do something for me   ⓑ a question

🎧 **B. Listen. Underline your response.**

1. (YOU) I have no idea.   (YOU) Yes. Would it be possible for you to close the door?

2. (YOU) As far as I know it is.   (YOU) Are you sure?

3. (YOU) I'm sorry. I didn't realize that.   (YOU) I'm glad to hear that.

🎧 **C. Listen again. Read your response out loud.**

🎧 **A.** Listening comprehension. **Listen to the conversations between neighbors.**

🎧 **B.** **Now listen to the conversations again and answer each question in your <u>own</u> words.**

Conversation 1

1. What's the problem? _____

2. What's the solution? _____

Conversation 2

1. What's the problem? _____

2. What's the solution? _____

C. True story. **Do you have a problem with a neighbor or co-worker? What's the problem? What have you done about it? What can you do about it? Tell your story to a partner.**

➤ Do it yourself!

A. **Write your <u>own</u> response. Then read your conversation out loud with a partner.**

Hi. Have you got a minute? I hate to complain, but I've got to make a request.

YOU _____

Last night when you were out, your kids played music until after midnight.

YOU _____

And this morning, there are pizza boxes and soda cans all over the place. Would it be possible for them to pick up some of that stuff?

YOU _____

B. Culture talk. **In the country you come from, is it easy or difficult to ask other people to be more considerate? Compare cultures with your classmates.**

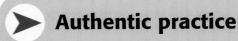
Awareness of community rules and laws

 A. Read and listen to the letters.

Ask Joan
Culture tips for newcomers

Dear Joan:

Every day I'm more surprised by my new country. Everything is against some rule or law!

I have a beautiful, friendly dog named Henry. It's difficult for a dog to live in a small apartment, and if he stays inside too much, he barks and bothers the neighbors. Henry loves to go to the park and run free. But yesterday a policeman gave me a ticket because he said I broke the leash law! Now I have to pay a $50 fine!

Joan, I don't think it's necessary to keep a dog on a leash all the time. Henry is a very friendly dog and he doesn't bother anyone. He always minds his own business.

Manuel in Manhattan

Dear Manuel:

I sympathize with you. It's hard to know all the rules and laws when you are a newcomer. Here are some things it's important to be aware of, no matter where you live:

- Most places have laws about animals. In most cities, you must have a license for a dog, you must keep the dog on a leash, and you must clean up any mess the dog leaves in the street.
- All states have laws that protect children from physical violence. And all states have laws about how old children must be to be left alone unsupervised at home.
- All states have laws about weapons, especially guns. Although laws differ from place to place, you must have a license for a gun, and there are laws about carrying guns and other weapons.
- All states have many laws about driving and parking, but the laws are often different in different places. For example, there are places where you may make a right turn after stopping at a red light and places where that is illegal.

Remember, above all: In this country, it is each person's responsibility to know what is legal and what is not legal. It's not acceptable to be unaware. So learn about the laws for the city and state where you live.

I'm sorry to hear that you got a ticket for the dog. But let the ticket be a lucky lesson and a warning to you to find out about the rules and the laws.

Joan

B. Check <u>True</u> or <u>False</u> for each statement.

	True	False
1. Laws are not the same everywhere.	☐	☐
2. Physical violence against children is illegal in this country.	☐	☐
3. It's illegal to have a gun anywhere in this country.	☐	☐
4. In some places it's OK to make a right turn at a red light.	☐	☐
5. If you don't know about a law, it's OK to break it.	☐	☐

C. What's your advice? Remember: Ignorance of the law is no excuse.

I want to buy a gun for protection. Do you know what the law is?

1. (YOU) _____

My neighbor asked my 10-year-old son to baby-sit. Isn't he too young? Do you know how old he has to be?

2. (YOU) _____

➤ Do it yourself!

A. Pair work. Talk about the signs. Talk about the people. Who is breaking the law? What are the penalties for the violations?

B. Discussion. Read the ticket. What is the violation? What does the person have to do?

COURT OF THE TOWN OF NEW CASTLE
APPEARANCE TICKET AND TRAFFIC INFORMATION

You are hereby charged with the following violation:

Comp. Code	Violation	Fine
01 ☐	No Parking Zone	
02 ☐	Meter Parking Violation	
03 ☐	Violation Leash Law	
04 ☑	No Helmet / Bike	$25.00
05 ☐	Littering	

PENALTY DOUBLES 30 DAYS AFTER ISSUE DATE. AFTER 60 DAYS FINE THEN INCREASES BY 1.5% PER MONTH.

DEFENDANT'S NAME _Grace Mullen_

DATE OF BIRTH _9_ / _17_ / _87_ /

ADDRESS _431 E. Greystone_
Monrovia, CA

ZIP _91016_

Review

A. Pair work or group work.

- What is happening?
- What are the problems?

Ask and answer questions.
Create conversations.
Tell a story.
Say as much as you can.

B. Listen to the conversations between co-workers. Read the statements and listen again. Check <u>True</u> or <u>False</u>.

	True	False
1. Smoking is against the office rules.	❑	❑
2. Harold smokes.	❑	❑
3. Nina's office has a door.	❑	❑
4. Nina asks Harold to smoke in the break room.	❑	❑

C. Complete each sentence.

1. In many towns you have to keep your dog on a _____.

2. Is it legal here to make a _____ on red?

3. They just got _____. They're going to get married in June.

4. Sam and Anne got _____. Now I hear they're getting a divorce.

5. She's upset because the factory closed and all the workers got _____.

D. Write a response to each statement.

1. "I can't stand all that noise! It's after midnight!"

   _____

2. "How are things?"

   _____

3. "My daughter's getting a divorce."

   _____

E. Write sentences and questions from the cues.

1. legal / park in a bus stop? _____

   _____

2. impolite / bother your co-workers with a lot of noise _____

   _____

3. important / be aware of the laws where you live _____

   _____

4. OK / play music late at night in this apartment house? _____

   _____

F. **Rewrite each sentence. Express the ideas in another way.**

1. <u>Knowing the laws where you live</u> is essential. _____

_____

2. <u>Having a gun without a license</u> is illegal. _____

_____

3. <u>Riding a bicycle without a helmet</u> is dangerous. _____

_____

4. In this state, is <u>having a dog without a license legal</u>? _____

_____

G. **Look at the ticket. Answer the questions.**

1. What is the violation?

_____

_____

_____

2. What does the person have to do?

_____

_____

_____

Notice of Parking Violation

Permit Displayed: No ☐ Yes ☐
____ Type ____   Rev. 12/00   N/A=Not Available

PLATE: H 6 5 5 R L   CD

DATE REGISTRATION EXPIRES
MO. 05   DAY 11   YR. 05

STATE: NY 1☐ CT 2☐ PA 3☐ NJ 4☐ MA 5☐ FL 6☒ OTHER
P TYPE: PAS 1☒ SRF 2☐ COM 3☐ OTHER ☐ N/A

MAKE: CEV 1☐ FORD 2☒ HONDA 3☐ DODGE 4☐ OLDS 5☐ BUICK 6☐ CADI 7☐ PONT 8☐ TOYT 9☐ NISSN 0☐ OTHER
COLOR Gr.   Yr. of Veh. 98

BODY TYPE: SEDAN 1☐ VAN 2☐ SUBN 3☒ DELV 4☐ OTHER   ALTERNATE PLATE   STATE

THE OPERATOR AND OWNER OF THE ABOVE VEHICLE ARE CHARGED AS FOLLOWS:

AM ☐ Time 3:17 PM ☒   Date of Offense 8/18/03   Time 1st Obsv'd A.M.☐ : P.M.☐   Date 1st Obsv'd   County

Front of ☒ 519 S. Winchester   Opposite ☐ Pct

Code	All Other Areas	Man. 96 St 7 So.	In Violation of Sect. 4/08 (subsect. below) of NYC Traffic Rules	Sign Restriction/ Other Information
14	☐ $55	☐ $55	No Standing (c)	Days in Effect ("ALL", unless otherwise stated):
16	☐ $55	☒ $55	No Standing except trucks (k) (2)	
17	☐ $55	☐ $55	No Standing except Auth. Vechicles (c) (4)	Hours in Effect ("ALL", unless otherwise stated):
18	☐ $55	☐ $55	No Standing Bus Stop (c) (3)	Fr: 8 ☒ A.M. ☐ P.M.
20	☐ $50	☐ $55	No Parking (d)	To: 6 ☐ A.M. ☒ P.M.
21	☐ $35	☐ $55	No Parking, SCR (d) (1)	Other Description/Rider

H. **Composition. On a separate sheet of paper, write about the picture on page 96. Say as much as you can.**

Now I can
☐ ask about and understand rules and laws.
☐ ask someone to be more considerate.
☐ apologize for inconsiderate behavior.
☐ understand personal responsibility to know and obey rules and laws.
☐ make small talk.
☐ congratulate someone on good news.
☐ express sympathy and offer to help.
☐ _____.

Your health and safety

> ## Preview

Warm up. What's the problem?

Unit 8 objectives

- Return food to a supermarket and explain why.
- Send food back in a restaurant and explain why.
- Give and understand directions for taking a medicine.
- Understand and apply food-safety techniques.
- Understand directions and warnings on medicines.

Model 1   Return an item to the supermarket. Provide a justification.

A. Listen and read.

A: Excuse me.

B: Yes?

A: I bought this meat here today, and its sell-by date is expired.

B: Would you like to get another package?

A: No, thanks. I'll just take a refund.

B: Certainly. Can I see your receipt?

A: Here you go.

B. Listen again and repeat.

Vocabulary

Reasons to return food to the store

It's not fresh.   It's spoiled.   Its sell-by date   It's marked wrong.
                                            is expired.

C. Pair work. Return something to the store. Use these items or your __own__ ideas.

    a package   a carton   a container   a loaf   a bag

A: Excuse me.

B: _____?

A: I bought _____, and _____.

B: Would you like to get another _____?

A: _____.

A. Listen and read.

A: Is everything OK?

B: Actually, this hamburger is not well done.

A: Oh, I'm sorry. Let me take it back. What about yours?

C: Mine's OK, thanks. But this milk's not fresh.

A: Oh, I'm so sorry. I'll take care of that right away.

B. Listen again and repeat.

Ways to order meat

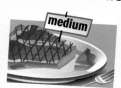

C. Group work. Complain about food that's not good, not fresh, or not the way you ordered it. Use your own ideas.

A: Is everything OK?

B: Actually, this _____ is not _____.

A: Oh, I'm sorry. Let me take it back. What about yours?

C: Mine's _____. But _____.

A: _____.

➤ Do it yourself!

A. Personalization. Have you ever returned something at a supermarket or restaurant? Complete the chart. Explain the problem. What did the supermarket or restaurant do?

Item	Problem	What happened?
milk	carton was open	The supermarket gave me another carton.

B. Pair work. Choose one item and use it to role-play a conversation between a customer and a manager or waiter/waitress.

Practical conversations

A. Listen and read.

A: I'm here to pick up a prescription.

B: Sure, Mr. Martinez.... It's ready.

A: Thanks. Oh, by the way, are the instructions on the label?

B: Yes. And there's more information on this patient information sheet.

B. Listen again and repeat.

Patient Information Sheet

Directions: TAKE 2 CAPSULES NOW, THEN 1 CAPSULE 3 TIMES DAILY.

IMPORTANT NOTE: THE FOLLOWING INFORMATION IS INTENDED TO SUPPLEMENT, NOT SUBSTITUTE FOR, THE EXPERTISE AND JUDGMENT OF YOUR PHYSICIAN, PHARMACIST, OR OTHER HEALTHCARE PROFESSIONAL.

IT SHOULD NOT BE CONSTRUED TO INDICATE THAT USE OF THE DRUG IS SAFE, APPROPRIATE, OR EFFECTIVE FOR YOU.

CONSULT YOUR HEALTHCARE PROFESSIONAL BEFORE USING THIS DRUG.

> Dr. Mila Ponti
> 625 First Ave.
> South Orange, NJ 07081
>
> Name: *Gloria Martinez*
>
> R₋ *For back pain,*
> *Percotrol 250mg tid*

Vocabulary

Important information about medications

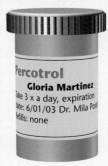

Percotrol
Gloria Martinez
Take 3 x a day, expiration
date: 6/01/03 Dr. Mila Ponti
Refills: none

Percotrol
Patient Information

Instructions: This medication is for pain. Take exactly as your doctor orders.

Dosage: The normal dose is 250 mg. three times a day.

Warnings: Do not take this medication if you are pregnant or nursing a baby.

Adverse reactions: Two percent of patients using Percotrol report flu-like symptoms.

C. Pair work. Pick up a prescription. Ask for information.

A: I'm here to pick up a prescription.

B: _____. . . . It's ready.

A: _____. Oh, by the way, _____ the _____ on the label?

B: _____.

A. Listen and read.

A: Here's the Percotrol for your back pain.
B: Thanks. What are the directions?
A: Take 1 capsule three times a day.
B: Three times a day?
A: That's right.

B. Listen again and repeat.

C. Pair work. Tell someone how to take medicine. Use the directions on these medications. Or use your <u>own</u> medications.

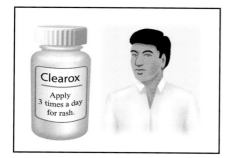

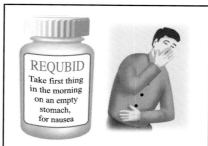

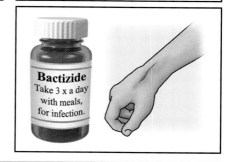

A: Here's the _____ for your _____.
B: Thanks. What are the directions?
A: _____.
B: _____?
A: That's right.

➤ Do it yourself!

A. Personalization. Complete the chart for medicines and other remedies you use.

Ailment	Medicine	Home remedy
the flu	aspirin	chicken soup
pain		
nausea		
rash		
other:		

B. Discussion. Compare medicines and remedies with a group.

Possession

> **Review the possessive adjectives.**
>   Evan takes **his** medicine before breakfast.
>   Jane takes **her** medicine before dinner.
>
> | <u>Subject pronouns</u> | <u>Possessive adjectives</u> |
> | --- | --- |
> | I | **my** |
> | you | **your** |
> | he | **his** |
> | she | **her** |
> | it | **its** |
> | we | **our** |
> | you | **your** |
> | they | **their** |

A. **Write the possessive adjective that corresponds to each subject pronoun.**

1. They usually get _____ food at the Magic Mart.

2. We'd like to return _____ hamburgers. They're not well done.

3. She doesn't know if _____ husband has any allergies.

4. Mr. Clark thinks _____ daughter needs to go to the doctor.

5. You need to bring _____ prescription with you.

> **Review the possessive nouns.**
>   Lewis**'s** son is allergic to penicillin.   The pharmacy**'s** hours are 8 a.m. to midnight.
>   The children**'s** doctor called the pharmacist.   The patients**'** appointments had to be changed.

B. **Complete each sentence with a possessive noun.**

1. ___*Roberto's*___ doctor prescribed medication for his flu.
        Roberto

2. The _____ instructions are on the prescription.
              doctor

3. We don't know the _____ side effects.
                        medication

4. _____ insomnia is better and she doesn't need medicine anymore.
        Joanna

5. The two _____ headaches are terrible.
                    brothers

No, I think it's **his**.

The yellow hard hat is **mine**. Is the blue one **yours**?

Possessive pronouns

Possessive pronouns are not followed by nouns. They stand alone.

This isn't your hard hat. It's **mine**.

Subject pronouns	Possessive adjectives	Possessive pronouns
I	my	**mine**
you	your	**yours**
he	his	**his**
she	her	**hers**
it	its	**its**
we	our	**ours**
you	your	**yours**
they	their	**theirs**

C. **Replace the words in parentheses with a possessive pronoun.**

1. Those prescriptions are (my prescriptions). _Those prescriptions are mine._

2. That penicillin is (his penicillin). _____

3. This rare hamburger is (your hamburger). _____

4. Is this patient information sheet (their patient information sheet)? _____
   _____

D. **Complete each sentence.**

1. _____ pharmacist can't fill this prescription right now.
   Ms. Elliot / Ms. Elliot's

2. I know _____ dinner is OK. What about _____?
   he / his   your / yours

3. Whose pharmacy is closer, _____ or _____?
   my / mine   their / theirs

➤ Do it yourself!

A. **Pair work. Create a conversation for the two men. Say as much as you can.**

B. **Discussion. Did you ever take something that belonged to someone else by mistake? Did anyone ever take anything of yours by mistake? Tell your story.**

Unit 8   105

➤ Authentic practice

🎧 A. Read and listen again. Then complete each statement. Fill in the ovals.

1. The restaurant is worried about _____.

   ⓐ meat safety   ⓑ fast food

2. Salmonella and *E. coli* are two types of _____.

   ⓐ undercooked meat   ⓑ dangerous bacteria

3. The cooks have to measure the meat's _____.

   ⓐ temperature   ⓑ bacteria

🎧 B. Listen. Underline your response.

1. (YOU) It's not fresh.   (YOU) Certainly not.

2. (YOU) Oh, I'm sorry. Let me take it back. (YOU) Can I make it rare?

3. (YOU) What about yours?   (YOU) Why? What's wrong?

🎧 C. Listen again. Read your response out loud.

🎧 **A.** **Listening comprehension.** **Listen to the public service announcement on the radio. Then answer the question in your own words.**

What's the purpose of the announcement? _____

_____

🎧 **B.** **Listen again. Listen for <u>Do's</u> and <u>Don'ts</u>. Check the boxes according to the advice.**

		Do	Don't
1.	Be aware of the danger of bacteria in warm weather.	☐	☐
2.	Leave food in the car.	☐	☐
3.	Wash hands after using the bathroom.	☐	☐
4.	Replace kitchen towels and sponges frequently.	☐	☐
5.	Thaw frozen food on the kitchen counter.	☐	☐

C. **True story.** **Do you know anyone who has had food poisoning? What was the cause? How can you prevent food poisoning? Tell your partner or your group.**

➤ Do it yourself!

A. **Write your <u>own</u> response. Give advice about food safety. Then read your conversation out loud with a partner.**

Hi. I'm running late. Could you please take the meat out of the freezer?

YOU _____

Please put the meat on the counter near the window. It's hot today, so it will defrost fast.

YOU _____

I already bought the chicken. I'll just keep it in the car while I pick up my prescription. Do you think that's OK?

YOU _____

B. **Culture talk.** **In the country you come from, how do you keep foods safe in warm weather? Compare cultures with your classmates.**

Over-the-counter (OTC) medications

A. Read the article about over-the-counter medications.

Pocket Digest

Educate yourself about OTCs

by Bonnie Crain, M.D.

Who's never had a cold? Where's the baby who hasn't suffered from teething woes, or the adult who hasn't had sore muscles or a headache, or an itchy rash from a food allergy?

No one gets through life without a little pain and suffering, not bad or serious enough to visit the doctor, but bad enough to seek relief on the pharmacy shelf.

What are OTCs?

Over-the-counter medicines, referred to as "OTCs," are medicines you can purchase without a doctor's prescription, simply by going to the nearest drugstore and choosing them yourself. Many of us make our choices based on word of mouth, advertisements, or by reading medicine package labels. Thousands of drugs are available over the counter, and it's important to be careful when choosing or taking them. Here are some important facts about OTCs:

1. OTCs are drugs. Just because they are available without a prescription doesn't mean they're harmless.
2. Many OTCs have side effects.
3. Mixing medications may be dangerous. Many OTCs can interact or interfere with the effects of your prescription drugs or with other OTCs.

How to use OTCs safely

Read package labels carefully. Be sure you understand warnings. Don't exceed the recommended dosage. When in doubt, ask the pharmacist or your doctor for advice. It's your responsibility, but the druggist and the doctor can help.

B. Answer the questions about over-the-counter drugs. Fill in the ovals.

1. What are OTCs?

   ⓐ medicines you buy without a prescription   ⓑ side effects

2. Where do you get OTCs?

   ⓐ at the drugstore   ⓑ from advertisements

3. What do OTCs do?

   ⓐ warn us   ⓑ treat ailments

4. What is a possible danger in using OTCs?

   ⓐ drug interactions   ⓑ lack of information

For extra practice, go to pages 159 and 160.

Directions and warnings on medicines

What's your advice? Read the package labels. Then tell each person what to do.

Alledrine
Antihistamine

For relief of the stuffy nose
and itchy eyes of seasonal allergies

Uses: Alleviates symptoms of seasonal allergies.
Directions: *See chart.*

Dosage	Age	First Dose	Next Dose	Maximum per day
Adults	12 and over	2 tablets	1 tablet	4 tablets

NOT RECOMMENDED FOR CHILDREN UNDER
12 YRS. CONSULT DOCTOR.

Warnings:
Do not use if you have a high fever (over 101°F).
Do not use if you are pregnant or nursing.
KEEP THIS AND ALL DRUGS OUT OF THE REACH OF
CHILDREN.
In case of accidental overdose, seek professional
assistance or call a poison control center immediately.

24 tablets   NEW

Lemon / Mint
ThroatEze

Extra Strength
With Kryptocaine

Anesthetic—for temporary relief of the pain of sore
throat due to colds and voice overuse.
Indications: For temporary relief of occasional throat
pain.
Directions: Adults and children over 2 years of age.
Allow disk to melt slowly in mouth. May be repeated
every 2 hours as needed or as directed by a physician.
Warnings: If condition is severe, persists for more
than 2 days, or is accompanied by fever, vomiting, or
rash, consult doctor promptly.

KEEP OUT OF THE REACH OF CHILDREN

Active ingredient: Each disk contains Kryptocaine
Hydrochloride 2.0 mg.

Made in USA.

24 sore throat disks

1. "My ten-year-old daughter has a stuffy nose and a high fever. Should I buy her
   Alledrine?" _____

2. "I have allergies every fall. I feel terrible. Do you think Alledrine will help?"
   _____

3. "Oh, my gosh. I read the package wrong. I took eight Alledrine tablets today.
   What should I do?" _____

4. "My throat is so sore I can hardly talk. Do you know anything that will help?"
   _____

5. "I've been taking ThroatEze for a week, but now I have a fever and a sore
   throat. Should I keep taking ThroatEze?" _____
   _____

➤ Do it yourself!

**Discussion. In your home country, are prescriptions necessary for all medications?
Who can write a prescription? Discuss other customs and laws for medications.**

Review

A. Pair work or group work.

- Where are the people?
- What are their problems?

Ask and answer questions.

Create conversations.

Tell a story.

Say as much as you can.

B. Listen to the conversations. Read the statements and listen again. Check <u>True</u> or <u>False</u>.

		True	False
1.	**Conversation 1.** They're talking about what to eat for breakfast.	☐	☐
2.	**Conversation 2.** They're discussing a sick child.	☐	☐
3.	**Conversation 3.** They're returning milk in a restaurant.	☐	☐

C. Look at the pictures of the ailments. Write the name of each ailment.

1. _____   2. _____   3. _____

D. Write a response to each statement or question.

1. **Manager:** Would you like to get another package?

   _____

2. **Waiter:** Is everything OK?

   _____

3. **Pharmacist:** Take one tablet three times a day.

   _____

4. **Co-worker:** I don't believe what you're doing!

   _____

5. **Boss:** They told you the policy, didn't they?

   _____

E. Complete each sentence with a possessive noun.

1. This is _____ prescription. Don't take it.

Edwin

2. My _____ daughter ate a rare hamburger and got food poisoning.

neighbor

3. The _____ label is missing, and I don't know how much to take.

medicine

4. The _____ appointments all had to be rescheduled.

patients

5. Dr. _____ office is closed today.

Klein

F. **Replace the words in parentheses with a possessive pronoun.**

1. That prescription for Bactizide is (my husband's prescription). _____

   _____

2. My hamburger is perfect. How's (your hamburger)? _____

   _____

3. These are his tablets. Where are (our tablets)? _____

   _____

4. My rash is better. What about (their rash)? _____

   _____

G. **Complete each sentence.**

1. _____ husband never takes Alledrine for his allergies.
   My / Mine

2. My appointment was rescheduled for tomorrow. What about _____?
   your / yours

3. Whose prescription is this, yours or _____?
   their / theirs

H. **Write two rules for safe food handling.**

1. _____

2. _____

I. **Composition. On a separate sheet of paper, write about the picture on page 110. Say as much as you can.**

Now I can
❏ return food to a supermarket and explain why.
❏ send food back in a restaurant and explain why.
❏ give and understand directions for taking a medicine.
❏ understand and apply food-safety techniques.
❏ understand directions and warnings on medicines.
❏ _____.

Your money

Preview

Warm up. What's the problem?

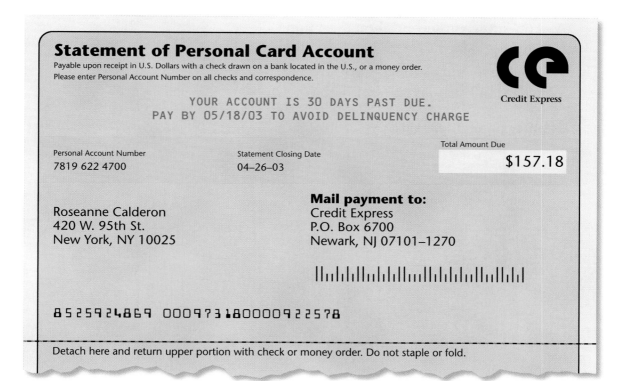

Statement of Personal Card Account

Payable upon receipt in U.S. Dollars with a check drawn on a bank located in the U.S., or a money order.
Please enter Personal Account Number on all checks and correspondence.

YOUR ACCOUNT IS 30 DAYS PAST DUE.
PAY BY 05/18/03 TO AVOID DELINQUENCY CHARGE

Credit Express

Personal Account Number
7819 622 4700

Statement Closing Date
04–26–03

Total Amount Due
$157.18

Roseanne Calderon
420 W. 95th St.
New York, NY 10025

Mail payment to:
Credit Express
P.O. Box 6700
Newark, NJ 07101–1270

8525924869 0009731800009225 78

Detach here and return upper portion with check or money order. Do not staple or fold.

Unit 9 objectives

- Discuss problems with debt.
- Find the appropriate person for financial information.
- Offer good and bad financial news.
- Complain about banking services.
- Express satisfaction and dissatisfaction.
- Get consumer advice for problems with debt.

Practical conversations

Model 1 Find the appropriate person for information. Decline an offer.

A. Listen and read.

> **A:** I'd like some information on mortgages. Are you the right person?
>
> **B:** Yes, I am. How can I help you?
>
> **A:** Can you tell me the current interest rate?
>
> **B:** Sure. It's 9.5%. Would you like a brochure?
>
> **A:** You know, on second thought, I think I'll shop around.
>
> **B:** Of course. But as long as you're here, why don't you take this along?

B. Listen again and repeat.

MORTGAGE
15 years $80,000
Interest 8%

Vocabulary

Bank services and accounts

loans

checking accounts and savings accounts

money market accounts certificates of deposit (CDs)

Money Market Account: **5.1%**
Interest Checking Account: **4.99%**
Passbook Savings Account: **4.00%**
6-month CD: **5.75%**

C. Pair work. Ask for information on interest rates. Decline an offer.

> **A:** I'd like some information on _____. Are you the right person?
>
> **B:** Yes, I am. _____?
>
> **A:** Can you tell me the current interest rate?
>
> **B:** _____. It's _____%. Would you like a brochure?
>
> **A:** You know, on second thought, I think I'll shop around.
>
> **B:** _____. But as long as you're here, why don't you take this along?

2%

10%

7.5%

3.75%

🎧 **A. Listen and read.**

A: Hi, Fred. How was your day?

B: Well, do you want the good news or the bad news?

A: Let's take the good news first.

B: Well, they approved our loan application.

A: That's good. So, what's the bad news?

B: We bounced three checks.

🎧 **B. Listen again and repeat.**

🎧 **Vocabulary**

Financial bad news	**Financial good news**
bounce a check	They approved our
be behind on your mortgage payments	loan application
have to pay a late fee	mortgage
have to pay a penalty	credit card application
have to pay finance charges	

C. Pair work. Talk about good and bad financial news.

A: Hi, _____. How was your day?

B: Well, do you want the good news or the bad news?

A: Let's take the _____ news first.

B: Well, _____.

A: That's _____. So, what's the _____ news?

B: _____.

➤ Do it yourself!

Discussion. What kinds of accounts do you have at the bank? What are the advantages and disadvantages of each kind of account?

Model 3 Put yourself in another's shoes. Discuss debt. Suggest the Yellow Pages.

🎧 **A.** **Listen and read.**

> **A:** I'm behind on my car payments.
> **B:** How far behind?
> **A:** Three months. And now they might repossess my car.
> **B:** Oh, no! How did that happen?
> **A:** Well, to tell you the truth, I got in over my head.
> **B:** If I were you, I'd check the Yellow Pages under "Credit Counseling." They help people get out of debt.

🎧 **B.** **Listen again and repeat.**

🎧 **Vocabulary**

Consequences of debt

I'm behind on my mortgage payments. They might foreclose on my house.

I'm behind on my rent. They might evict me.

I'm behind on my car payments. They might repossess my car.

I'm behind on my credit card payments. They might cancel my card.

C. Pair work. **A friend is in debt. Suggest checking the Yellow Pages or calling one of the counseling services below. Or make your own suggestion.**

> **A:** I'm behind on my _____.
> **B:** How far behind?
> **A:** _____. And now they might _____.
> **B:** Oh, no! How did that happen?
> **A:** Well, to tell you the truth, I got in over my head.
> **B:** If I were you, I'd _____.

CREDIT AND DEBT COUNSELING SVCES.

In debt? Need Help?
Help is a phone call away.
Call **1-800-NO-DEBTS**
Stop those harassing calls.
Consolidate your bills into
one affordable monthly payment.

Drowning in debt? In over your head?
Creditors calling?
Call **1-800-555-HELP** or
Log on to overmyhead.com

A. Listen and read.

A: Marie, I want to change banks.

B: How come?

A: Well, my bank keeps raising fees. I've had enough! Where do you bank?

B: At Green Tree. I'm satisfied with the service there. If I were you, I'd change to Green Tree.

B. Listen again and repeat.

Dissatisfaction
I've had enough!
I'm fed up!
I've had it!

Satisfaction
satisfied
pretty happy
pleased

Vocabulary

Complaints about bank services

MONEY BUSH BANK

Dear Client:
We're sorry to inform you that as of April 1, fees on all accounts will go up 2%. We take this measure in order to

Interest Checking 3.8%
Interest Checking 4.5%

MONEY BUSH BANK

Dear Client:
Effective immediately, we no longer offer free checking or free traveler's checks. We are sorry for this inconvenience

Jones Street Branch closed. Please use Smith Street Branch.

raise fees   lower interest rates   reduce services   close branch offices

C. Pair work. Express dissatisfaction with your bank. Advise your partner.

A: _____, I want to change banks.

B: _____?

A: Well, my bank keeps _____. I _____! Where do you bank?

B: At _____. I'm _____ there. If I were you, I'd change to _____.

➤ Do it yourself!

A. Look up "Credit and Debt Counseling Services" in the Yellow Pages. Write the names of two services. What does each service _say_ it can do for you?

Credit Counseling of Hudson Valley: "Tired of seeing red? Get in the black."
1.
2.

B. Discussion. Talk about the claims each service makes. Explain what it means.

Conditional sentences

If we **banked** at Global Bank, we **would get** free checking.

True. But we don't bank at Global.

Unreal conditions and results

condition that doesn't exist   result

If we **banked** at Global Bank, we **would get** free checking. (But we don't bank at Global Bank, so we don't get free checking.)

Use _if_ and a past tense form for a condition that doesn't exist.

If we **got** behind on our car payments, they would repossess the car.

Use _if_ and _were_ for all forms of _be_.

I'd change to Green Bank **if** I **were** you.

Use _would_ and a verb to show the result.

If we weren't happy at our bank, we**'d go** to another one.

we**'d** = we would

A. Check the statements that describe conditions that don't exist.

1. ☐ We banked at Global Bank last year, and we got a higher interest rate.

2. ☐ If we banked at Global Bank, we'd get a higher interest rate.

3. ☐ When we applied for a mortgage, they asked us how much money we needed.

4. ☐ If I were you, I would complain.

B. Complete each unreal conditional sentence.

1. If we ___were___ in debt, we'_d call___ a credit counseling service.
      be   call

2. What _____ you _____ if your boss _____ you?
                        do   not pay

3. If people _____ more careful, they _____ in over their heads.
              be   not get

4. If I _____ a loan, I'_____ about the interest rate.
        need   ask

5. We _____ a joint checking account if we _____ married.
        not have   not be

6. If I _____ a good job, I _____ that car.
        not have   not buy

Keep and gerund

Again! Money Bush **keeps raising** the fees on checking accounts. I've had enough.

Let's change to Green Tree.

Use <u>keep</u> and a gerund to describe an action that continues and might not stop.

Sven **keeps buying** things he can't afford. He needs to get out of debt.

C. **Complete the sentences about continuing actions with <u>keep</u> and gerunds.**

1. John and Elena _____ checks. They have to pay a penalty too.
   bounce

2. They _____ the rent late, so they always pay a late fee.
   pay

3. We _____ at Money Bush, but the service is terrible.
   bank

4. Why do they _____ about the service? They should just change banks.
   complain

5. She _____ her whole paycheck, so she doesn't save any money.
   spend

6. It's bad to _____ in debt. We shouldn't buy that new car.
   get

➤ Do it yourself!

A. Pair work. **Write three questions to ask your classmates.**

1. What would you do if _____?

2. What would you do if _____?

3. What would you do if _____?

B. Discussion. **Talk about the most interesting answers.**

Authentic practice

🎧 **A. Read and listen again. Then choose the sentence closer in meaning. Fill in the ovals.**

1. "It keeps you from spending more than you have."

    ⓐ It makes you keep spending, no matter how much money you have.

    ⓑ It prevents you from getting in over your head.

2. "Credit cards are an invitation to live beyond your means."

    ⓐ Credit cards encourage you to spend more than you have.

    ⓑ Credit cards help you stay out of debt.

3. "If I were in your shoes, I'd get myself a debit card."

    ⓐ I'd buy those shoes for myself if I had a debit card.

    ⓑ If I were you, I would use a debit card too.

🎧 **B. Listen. Underline your response.**

1. (YOU) If you had a debit card, you wouldn't spend more than you had.   (YOU) Oh, good. I don't want to get in over my head.

2. (YOU) Well, you can really get into debt.   (YOU) Let's take the good news first.

3. (YOU) What's the bad news?   (YOU) So don't keep using that credit card.

🎧 **C. Listen again. Read your response out loud.**

A. Listening comprehension. **Listen to the conversations about credit. Then read the questions and listen again. Answer the questions.**

Conversation 1

1. What's the offer for? _____

2. What are some reasons she thinks it's a good offer? _____

3. Why should you always read the fine print? _____

Conversation 2

1. What's the offer for? _____

2. What are some reasons he thinks it's a good offer? _____

3. Why should you always read the fine print? _____

B. True story. **Did you ever see an offer that was too good to be true? What was it for? Where did you see it?** *Was* **it too good to be true? Tell your partner or your group.**

For extra practice, go to page 161.

➤ Do it yourself!

A. Write your **own** response. **Then read your conversation out loud with a partner.**

I'm already in debt, but these new cards sound better than the one I use. What do you think?

(YOU) _____

Someone told me to get a debit card. This might be a silly question, but what is that exactly?

(YOU) _____

What would you do if you were in my shoes?

(YOU) _____

B. Culture talk. **In the country you come from, how do you get help when you're in debt? Compare cultures with your classmates.**

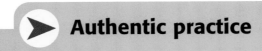

Authentic practice

Consumer advice for problems with debt

A. Read this information about debt from the U.S. Federal Trade Commission's Web site.

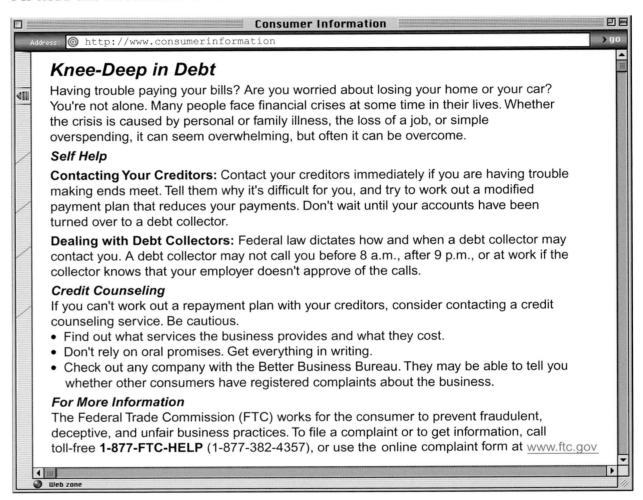

Consumer Information

Address: http://www.consumerinformation

Knee-Deep in Debt

Having trouble paying your bills? Are you worried about losing your home or your car? You're not alone. Many people face financial crises at some time in their lives. Whether the crisis is caused by personal or family illness, the loss of a job, or simple overspending, it can seem overwhelming, but often it can be overcome.

Self Help

Contacting Your Creditors: Contact your creditors immediately if you are having trouble making ends meet. Tell them why it's difficult for you, and try to work out a modified payment plan that reduces your payments. Don't wait until your accounts have been turned over to a debt collector.

Dealing with Debt Collectors: Federal law dictates how and when a debt collector may contact you. A debt collector may not call you before 8 a.m., after 9 p.m., or at work if the collector knows that your employer doesn't approve of the calls.

Credit Counseling

If you can't work out a repayment plan with your creditors, consider contacting a credit counseling service. Be cautious.
- Find out what services the business provides and what they cost.
- Don't rely on oral promises. Get everything in writing.
- Check out any company with the Better Business Bureau. They may be able to tell you whether other consumers have registered complaints about the business.

For More Information

The Federal Trade Commission (FTC) works for the consumer to prevent fraudulent, deceptive, and unfair business practices. To file a complaint or to get information, call toll-free **1-877-FTC-HELP** (1-877-382-4357), or use the online complaint form at www.ftc.gov

Web zone

B. Complete each sentence with the phrase closer in meaning to the underlined word or phrase. Fill in the ovals.

1. Whether the crisis is caused by personal or family illness, the loss of a job, or simple <u>overspending</u>, it can seem overwhelming, but often can be overcome.

   ⓐ spending more money than you have   ⓑ spending less money than you have

2. Contact your creditors immediately if you are having trouble <u>making ends meet</u>.

   ⓐ living within your means   ⓑ getting in over your head

C. Answer the questions in your <u>own</u> words.

1. What is debt? _____

2. What are some solutions to debt? _____

_____

Credit card bills

A. Read the credit card bill. If this were your bill, how much would you pay? Write a check.

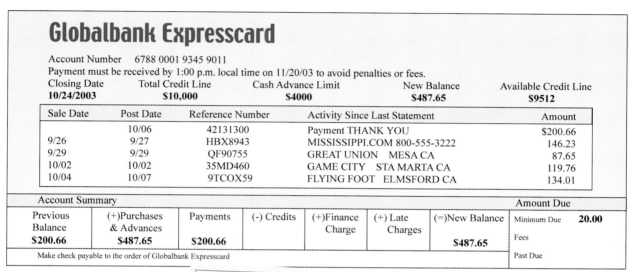

B. Answer the questions.

1. When does Globalbank have to receive the check so that the client doesn't have

   to pay a late fee? _____

2. Did the client pay last month's bill in full? _____

➤ Do it yourself!

Discussion. How much did you pay? Was that the full amount? Why? Explain the reason for your decision.

> # ► Review
>
> ## A. Pair work or group work.
>
> - Where are the people?
> - What are they doing?
>
> Ask and answer questions.
>
> Create conversations.
>
> Tell a story.
>
> Say as much as you can.

B. Listen to the conversation. Listen again and check the good news about checking accounts at Express Bank.

1. ☐ free microwave oven
2. ☐ free trips to national parks
3. ☐ no fees for the first year
4. ☐ no-bounce checking

5. ☐ no minimum balance
6. ☐ high interest on balance
7. ☐ valid at branches nearby

C. Write your own response.

1. "I'm behind on my credit card payments." _____

   _____

2. "I was living beyond my means and I got in over my head." _____

   _____

3. "This might be a silly question, but what's the difference between a credit card and a debit card?" _____

   _____

D. Complete each unreal conditional sentence with the appropriate words. Choose verbs from the box.

| forget | evict | get | cancel |

1. If I got behind on my rent, they _____ me.
2. If I didn't pay my credit card bill, they _____ my card.
3. If I _____ to send in my car payments for a couple of months, they'd repossess my car.
4. If I _____ behind on my mortgage payments, they'd foreclose on my house.

E. Complete the sentences about continuing actions with keep and gerunds.

1. They _____ me these bills. What should I do?

send

2. Don't _____ this credit card, or you'll get in over your head.

use

3. Elsa _____ me to read the fine print. She's right.

tell

4. My bank _____ fees and lowering interest rates!

raise

F. **Read the credit card bill. Write a check for the full amount.**

HANDICard

Account Summary							Amount Due
Previous Balance	(+)Purchases & Advances	Payments	(−)Credits	(+)Finance Charge	(+)Late Charges	(=)New Balance	Minimum Due **20.00** Fees Past Due
166.32	340.97	166.32				340.97	

Make check payable to the order of HandiCard

890

Date _____

PAY TO THE ORDER OF _____ $ [_____]

THE SUM OF _____ Dollars

Second National Bank
270 Beltway
Mountainview, NY 10549

MEMO _____

021000021^^:4535*/"■890

G. Composition. **On a separate sheet of paper, write about the picture on page 124. Say as much as you can.**

Now I can
❑ discuss problems with debt.
❑ find the appropriate person for financial information.
❑ offer good and bad financial news.
❑ complain about banking services.
❑ express satisfaction and dissatisfaction.
❑ get consumer advice for problems with debt.
❑ _____.

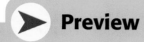

Preview

Warm up. What do you have to do to apply for these jobs? Talk with a partner.

Unit 10 objectives

- Respond to a classified job ad.
- Call for an interview.
- Talk about job history and references at an interview.
- Move to a first-name basis.
- Accept and respond to feedback on the job.

Model 1   Call for an interview.

🎧 **A.** **Listen and read.**

A: Hello. My name is Angela Andrade. I'm calling about the ad for a purchaser in today's paper.

B: Yes, Ms. Andrade. Could you fax me your job history and salary requirements?

A: Sure.

B: Please send it to my attention. I'm Roseanne Leon.

🎧 **B.** **Listen again and repeat.**

1-800-555-2

PURCHASER
CALL Roseanne Leon
at 723-2000 or
FAX 723-2100.

C. Pair work. **Call for an interview for one of these jobs. Or find an ad in your newspaper and role-play a call. Use your <u>own</u> names.**

555-7890

IMMEDIATE
OPENING
MEDICAL BILLER
Wanted for busy NJ office.
Must have experience in
Windows-based system.
Fax 222 6745
ATTN: Human Resources

★ **CHEF MANAGER** ★
Exp'd, limited nites. Good
pay. Private club.
Call 685 9800

A: Hello. My name is _____. I'm calling about the ad for _____ in today's paper.

B: Yes, _____. Could you fax me your job history and salary requirements?

A: _____.

B: Please send it to my attention. I'm _____.

A. Listen and read.

A: So, Mr. Chavez, who was your last employer?

B: I worked at Carmody Cleaners for two years.

A: And why did you leave that job?

B: Actually, they closed the shop.

A: Do you have a reference?

B: Yes, Mr. White. I can give you a list.

A: May we contact them?

B: Of course.

B. Listen again and repeat.

Vocabulary

Reasons to change jobs or to leave a job

So, why did you leave your last job?

They closed.

They moved to a new location.

There were no opportunities for me to advance.

The hours were not good for me.

I needed full-time / part-time employment.

I had a personality conflict with my _____.

C. Pair work. Explain why you left your last job. Provide references.

A: So, _____, who was your last employer?

B: I worked _____.

A: And why did you leave that job?

B: Actually, _____.

A: Do you have a reference?

B: Yes, _____.

A: May we contact _____?

B: _____.

➤ Do it yourself!

Pair work. Create an interview for the two people in the picture.

Practical conversations

🎧 **A. Listen and read.**

> **A:** Have you got a minute?
> **B:** Sure.
> **A:** I've been meaning to tell you, Dan. You're doing a great job.
> **B:** Really? Thanks, Mr. Meland. I'm happy to hear that.
> **A:** Thank *you*. By the way, please call me Jerry.

🎧 **B. Listen again and repeat.**

🎧 **Ways to move to a first-name basis**

Please call me Jerry.
Why don't you call me Jerry?
I think it's time you called me Jerry.
Just call me Jerry.

🎧 **Vocabulary**

Ways to accept positive feedback at work

You're doing a great job.

Really? Thanks.   I am? Thanks.

Thanks. I'm happy to hear that.

C. Pair work. Accept a compliment on your work. Use your <u>own</u> names. Move to a first-name basis.

> **A:** Have you got a minute?
> **B:** _____.
> **A:** I've been meaning to tell you, _____. You're doing a _____ job.
> **B:** _____. I'm happy to hear that.
> **A:** Thank *you*. By the way, _____.

🎧 **A.** **Listen and read.**

A: Have you had a chance to read your review yet?

B: Yes, I have.

A: You've had a really good first year with us, Phil.

B: Thanks, Rob.

A: Where do you see yourself in two years?

B: Well, I'm interested in being a supervisor.

A: Great. Let's see if we can get you some training.

PERFORMANCE REVIEW

BUSINESS UNIT:	Brimstone Tire, Tulsa
EMPLOYEE NAME:	Philip Lee
REVIEW PERIOD:	2003

🎧 **B.** **Listen again and repeat.**

🎧 **Vocabulary**

Ways to advance on the job

training

hands-on experience

extra experience

on-the-job training

C. **Pair work.** **Discuss career goals. Use your <u>own</u> goal and names.**

A: Have you had a chance to read your review yet?

B: _____.

A: You've had a really good _____ with us, _____.

B: _____.

A: Where do you see yourself _____?

B: Well, I'm interested in being _____.

A: _____. Let's see if we can get you some _____.

➤ Do it yourself!

A. **Personalization.** **Where do you see yourself in the future? Complete the bottom of the performance review form.**

B. **Discussion.** **Discuss career goals with a partner or a group.**

Evaluation: _Excellent work._

What are your career goals for the next five years?

_____

_____

_____

Talking about the present: Review

Use the simple present tense for general statements and to describe habitual actions.
   The office **opens** at 9:00.
   He **goes** to work at 7:30.
Use the simple present tense with frequency adverbs.
   I usually **get** to work on time.
Use the simple present tense with <u>have</u>, <u>want</u>, <u>need</u>, and <u>like</u>.
   She **doesn't like** her job.

Use the present continuous for actions in progress. Don't use it with frequency adverbs. Don't use it with <u>have</u>, <u>want</u>, <u>need</u>, or <u>like</u>.
   She's **talking** to the interviewer right now, but she doesn't need a job.

A. Choose the simple present tense or the present continuous.

1. I can't talk to you right now. I _____ my performance review.
   read / am reading

2. I _____ a few important questions to ask at the interview.
   have / am having

3. Usually I work at an office, but today I _____ at home.
   work / am working

4. Ivan _____ to his supervisor once a week.
   talks / is talking

5. It always _____ when I have a day off!
   rains / is raining

B. Complete each sentence with the simple present tense or the present continuous.

1. They always _____ job applicants for references.
   ask

2. He _____ his supervisor.
   not like

3. Look at Nan fixing that copier. She _____ a great job! Let's go tell her.
   do

4. That interviewer never _____ the interview on time.
   end

5. I _____ to fax a letter to them. What's their fax number?
   need

Actions that started in the past and continue in the present

Use the present perfect or the present perfect continuous with <u>for</u> and <u>since</u> to talk about actions that started in the past and continue in the present. For this purpose the two forms mean almost the same thing.

I**'ve worked** here **since** August, 2000. (present perfect)

She**'s been talking** to the interviewer **for** an hour. (present perfect continuous)

Remember: <u>for</u> + amounts of time.

Remember: <u>since</u> + a specific day, month, year, time, or date.

Be careful! Don't use the present continuous with <u>for</u> and <u>since</u>.

C. **Matt Joong is applying for a job. Complete the response letter he faxed.**

Sir or Madam: April 4, 2003

_____ to respond to the ad _____ for an
   1. I write / I'm writing   2. you have / you have had

electronics technician in today's *Journal News*. Currently _____
                                                                          3. I work / I have been working

at Sparky's Computer Repair. _____ there since May 1999. At
                                          4. I'm working / I've been working

Sparky's _____ computers. Sparky's always _____
              5. I'm repairing / I repair   6. treats / is treating

me well. But, unfortunately, Sparky's _____ no opportunities for
                                                      7. has / is having

advancement, and the management never _____ on-the-job training.
                                                        8. provides / is providing

For that reason, for the last month, _____ electronics at the
                                                  9. I study / I've been studying

Claremont Technical School.

If you would like me to come in for an interview, you can reach me at 322-2121 any
day after 5:30. I'm enclosing a job history and a list of references. I look forward
to hearing from you.

Sincerely,

Matt Joong

Matt Joong
Attachments

➤ Do it yourself!

A. **Pair work. Ask questions about your partner's job history or residence.**

Where are you currently employed?

How long have you lived at that address?

B. **Discussion. Talk about the job and housing history of your classmates.**

Unit 10   133

🎧 **A. Read and listen again. Answer the questions in your <u>own</u> words. Then discuss with a partner or a group.**

1. Has Sam done a good job this quarter? _____

2. What is Jerry's opinion of Sam's work? _____

3. What should Sam do to improve his "people skills"? _____

   _____

4. Why do you think it is important to show appreciation? _____

   _____

🎧 **B. Listen. Underline <u>your</u> response.**

1. (YOU) Really? I'm happy to hear that.　(YOU) I can give you a list.

2. (YOU) Has there been a problem?　(YOU) Can I fax you my resume?

3. (YOU) I'll send it to your attention.　(YOU) That's good advice. Thanks.

🎧 **C. Listen again. Read <u>your</u> response out loud.**

🎧 **A.** Listening comprehension. **Listen to the job tips.**

🎧 **B.** Read the following job tips. Listen again and check the tips the speaker advises.

1. ☐ Wear nice clothes to the interview.
2. ☐ Call the interviewer by his or her last name.
3. ☐ Make small talk about the weather.
4. ☐ Don't look relaxed.
5. ☐ Don't ask questions about the company or the job.
6. ☐ Be sure to ask about company benefits before the interviewer mentions them.

C. True story. **Have you ever had a job interview? What questions did the interviewer ask? What questions did you ask about the company or job? Tell your partner or your group.**

➤ Do it yourself!

A. Write your <u>own</u> response. Then read your interview out loud with a partner.

> How did you hear about this position?

YOU _____

> Please tell me something about your current job or work history.

YOU _____

> What would you like to ask me?

YOU _____

B. Culture talk. **In the country you come from, how do you accept and respond to negative feedback from a supervisor? Compare cultures with your classmates.**

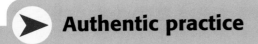

Friendliness and familiarity with an employer

🎧 **A.** **Read and listen to the letters.**

Ask Joan
Culture tips for newcomers

Dear Joan:
I have been working in this country since last year, and I've had a job in a fast-food restaurant for about three months. Yesterday I had my first performance review with my boss. He said, "Andy, you're doing a great job. We're very happy with you. We're looking forward to having you work with us for a long time!" I went home feeling great about my new country.

Then today something terrible happened. I was cleaning up the grill at about 5 after 5. My boss saw me and said, "Andy! Go home. Get out of here!"

What happened? What is wrong with the people in this country? I'll never understand. Maybe I should just go home to my country.

Andy in Anaheim

Dear Andy:
Stop worrying! When your boss told you to go home, he was letting you know that he recognized that you're willing to work long hours for him. He wanted to let you know how much he appreciates your effort. He wanted you to know that you had worked enough for one day.

Sometimes it's easier for people to say something in the joking way your boss did than to tell you directly. Your boss wanted to let you know that your relationship has become more friendly and less formal.

In the culture of this country, this is normal and good! The next time this happens, smile and say, "Thanks! I'll just finish the grill and then leave." This will let your boss know you understand the "message."

Congratulations on the good review. And best of luck for continued success in the job.

Joan

B. **Mark each statement <u>True</u> or <u>False</u>.**

		True	False
1.	Andy has worked at the fast-food restaurant for a year.	❑	❑
2.	Andy's boss is satisfied with Andy's work.	❑	❑
3.	Andy thinks his boss is angry at him.	❑	❑
4.	Andy's boss *was* angry.	❑	❑
5.	Andy's boss wants him to return home to his country.	❑	❑

C. **Discussion. First write answers. Then discuss with your classmates.**

1. What's Andy worried about? _____

2. What's Joan's explanation? _____

3. Has anyone ever said anything to you that caused a misunderstanding like
   Andy's? Explain. _____

Letters of response to job ads

A. **Read the job ad and the response letter.**

PICTURE FRAMER

Custom Picture Framing Co.
Located in Plainesville
Seeking fitters and other
production personnel.
Excellent salary and full
union benefits. Fax resume
or letter to Mr. Page at
845-555-7654.

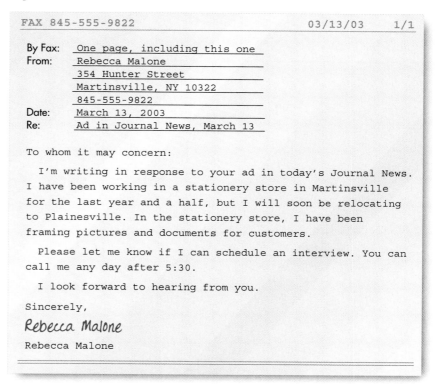

FAX 845-555-9822   03/13/03   1/1

By Fax: One page, including this one
From: Rebecca Malone
          354 Hunter Street
          Martinsville, NY 10322
          845-555-9822
Date: March 13, 2003
Re: Ad in Journal News, March 13

To whom it may concern:

    I'm writing in response to your ad in today's Journal News.
I have been working in a stationery store in Martinsville
for the last year and a half, but I will soon be relocating
to Plainesville. In the stationery store, I have been
framing pictures and documents for customers.

    Please let me know if I can schedule an interview. You can
call me any day after 5:30.

    I look forward to hearing from you.

Sincerely,

Rebecca Malone

Rebecca Malone

B. **Role play. Role-play a telephone conversation between Ms. Malone and Mr. Page. Discuss skills, experience, and references.**

➤ Do it yourself!

Read the ads. Then write a letter in response to one of the jobs. Use a separate sheet of paper.

★ **MANICURIST** ★

Exp'd manicurists at Galleria
of White Plains. Perform all
nail services. Must speak
fluent English. Contact Mary
at 602-555-7899 or FAX 602-
555-7890

Help Wanted

Automotive Manager
OIL CHANGE
$30K+
A new 4-bay lube facility
opening in Brewster is looking for a key person with
auto exp. Call Mr. George at
415-555-6432 or fax 415-555-
6400, Mon-Fri, 9-5.

For extra practice, go to page 162.

Review

A. Pair work or group work.

- Who are the people?
- Tell the story of the wife's job.

Ask and answer questions.

Create conversations.

Tell a story.

Say as much as you can.

B. Listen to the job interview. Read the statements and listen again. Check the mistakes Ms. Chung made.

1. ☐ She was late.

2. ☐ She was too familiar with the interviewer.

3. ☐ She talked too much about herself.

4. ☐ She asked about the salary too soon.

5. ☐ She didn't ask a question about the company.

C. Complete the letter about Mark's recent activities.

Hi, Frank,

Well, I'm sorry I _____ for a while. I am very
             1. haven't written / am not writing

busy and I never _____ any time anymore. Let
             2. have / have had

me bring you up to date. I _____ in this new
             3. am living / 've been living

apartment for about three weeks, and I _____ it
             4. like / am liking

very much. I _____ new furniture and a new
             5. need / have been needing

refrigerator, but that's nothing. What I really _____
             6. am wanting / want

is a new job. I _____ at the local supermarket
             7. 've been working / 'm working

for about six months, and that's six months too long! The manager

never _____ anything good that I do. I don't
             8. is noticing / notices

feel appreciated, and I'm fed up! Tonight I _____
             9. am having / have

an interview for a new job, and I'll let you know how it goes.

In a hurry!

Mark

D. **Read each statement or question. Write your <u>own</u> response.**

1. "Why did you leave your last job?" _____

   _____

2. "I've been meaning to tell you — we're very satisfied with your work." _____

   _____

3. "Where do you see yourself in a year?" _____

   _____

4. "I think it's time we moved to a first-name basis." _____

   _____

E. Composition. **On a separate sheet of paper, write about the picture on page 138. Say as much as you can.**

Now I can
- ❑ respond to a classified job ad.
- ❑ call for an interview.
- ❑ talk about job history and references at an interview.
- ❑ move to a first-name basis.
- ❑ accept and respond to feedback on the job.
- ❑ _____.

This is an alphabetical list of all active vocabulary in *Workplace Plus 3*. The numbers refer to the page on which the word first appears. When a word has two meanings (a new <u>brush</u> OR <u>Brush</u> your hair), both are in the list.

This is a unit-by-unit list of all the social language from the practical conversations in *Workplace Plus 3*.

Unit 1

Model 1

Nice weather today.
You know, I don't think we've met.
Nice to meet you.
Nice to meet you too.
By the way, . . .
You do?
Thanks!

Model 2

That's incredible!
That's amazing!
You're kidding!
Wow! It's a small world.

Model 3

Could you do me a favor?
Of course.
I need a reference.
Would you mind _____ing . . . ?
Not at all.
I'd be glad to.
Thanks so much.
I appreciate it.

Model 4

Tell me something about yourself.
I'm pretty good / not very good at that.
Actually, . . .

Unit 2

Model 1

Excuse me.
Can you tell me how to get to _____?
Sure.
Go straight.
Turn right / left.
Make a right / left.
Make your (second) left / right.
Go down the hall.
Go to the end of the hall.

Go up / down the stairs.
Take the escalator / the elevator.

Model 2

Hold the elevator, please!
Going up?
There you go.

Model 3

Hello. (to answer the phone)
Could you please tell me how to get there?
I'm taking the bus / train / subway.
At the corner of _____ and _____.
Take the number _____ to _____ and transfer
    there to the _____.
OK.
It's right on the corner.
You can't miss it.

Model 4

I was wondering, . . .
Would you like to _____ sometime?
We'd love to.
That would be nice.
Sounds great.
Yes. Let's do that!
When would be good?
How about _____?
Around _____ o'clock?
That's fine.
Why don't we _____?

Unit 3

Model 1

I wonder if this _____ is still under warranty.
No problem.

Model 2

Uh-oh.
I'm going to get in trouble.
What do you mean?
Don't worry.
It's always good to speak up.

Model 3

Can you believe it?

That's ridiculous.

What a waste of time!

You can say that again!

Model 4

What's the matter?

My computer is down / is frozen / crashed.

But that didn't help.

Unit 4

Model 1

Could you have a look at _____?

Well, no wonder.

They're not up to code / not too good / below standard.

Model 2

Do you carry _____?

That's a shame.

Really?

Would you like to have a look?

Model 3

I'm sorry, those were discontinued / didn't meet EPA rules.

That's too bad.

Model 4

How can I help you?

I heard there's been a recall.

Please bring it in and we'll give you a replacement.

Can I get a credit instead?

Absolutely. So long as you have your receipt.

Unit 5

Model 1

Tell me, what are you doing these days?

I'm working as _____.

That's great!

How are you paid?

By the hour / job / week / trip.

By the hour, plus room and board / plus tips.

Model 2

What are the hours?

We pay minimum wage / time and a half for overtime / double time.

Could you repeat that, please? I'd like to make a note of it.

Model 3

I'm sorry, but I have to reschedule.

How's _____?

Actually, that won't work.

Yeah. That's good for me.

Model 4

Is that a problem / an emergency?

No, not really.

Why don't you do that at lunch time / at break time / after closing time?

Unit 6

Model 1

What a bargain!

That must be a mistake.

Model 2

Can I make a suggestion?

Call _____ or log on to _____.

Hey, why didn't *I* think of that?

Unit 7

Model 1

Would it be possible for you to _____?

It's after _____ o'clock.

Oh, I'm sorry. I didn't realize that.

You're welcome.

Model 2

Is it legal to _____?

Well, to tell you the truth, I'm not sure / not positive / I have no idea.

As far as I know, it is.

Model 3

How are things?

How's it going?

How're you doing?

How are you?

What's up?
What's new?
Pretty good.
How about you?
Great, actually.
Congratulations.
I'm really happy to hear that.

Model 4

You look upset.
Is there anything wrong?
Well, actually, _____.
Oh, I'm so sorry to hear that.
Is there anything I can do?
Thanks for offering.

Unit 8

Model 1

Yes?
No, thanks.
I'll just take a refund.
Certainly.
Can I see your receipt?
Here you go.

Model 2

Is everything OK?
Actually, this _____ is not _____.
Let me take it back.
Oh, I'm so sorry. I'll take care of that right away.

Model 3

I'm here to _____.
Oh, by the way, _____?

Model 4

Here's _____.
That's right.

Unit 9

Model 1

I'd like some information on _____.
Are you the right person?
Can you tell me the _____?
You know, on second thought, I think I'll shop around.
Of course.

But as long as you're here, why don't you _____?

Model 2

How was your day?
Do you want the good news or the bad news?
Let's take the good news first.
That's good.
So, what's the bad news?

Model 3

Be behind on _____.
Oh, no! How did that happen?
I got in over my head.
If I were you, I'd _____.

Model 4

How come?
I've had enough!
I'm fed up!
I've had it!
I'm pretty happy.

Unit 10

Model 1

I'm calling about the ad for _____ in today's paper.
Could you fax me _____?
Please send it to my attention.

Model 3

Have you got a minute?
I've been meaning to tell you, . . .
You're doing a great job.
Really? Thanks.
I am? Thanks.
Thanks. I'm happy to hear that.
Thank *you*.
By the way, please call me _____.
Why don't you call me _____?
I think it's time you called me _____.
Just call me _____.

Model 4

Have you had a chance to _____?
You've had a really good _____ with us.
Where do you see yourself in (two) years?
Well, I'm interested in being _____.
Let's see if we can get you some _____.

The following verbs from *Workplace Plus 3* have irregular past-tense forms.

Base form	Past-tense form	Past participle
be	was / were	been
begin	began	begun
break	broke	broken
bring	brought	brought
buy	bought	bought
can	could	been able to
choose	chose	chosen
come	came	come
do	did	done
drink	drank	drunk
drive	drove	driven
eat	ate	eaten
fall	fell	fallen
fight	fought	fought
find	found	found
forget	forgot	forgotten
get	got	gotten
give	gave	given
go	went	gone
have	had	had
hear	heard	heard
hurt	hurt	hurt
know	knew	known
leave	left	left
let	let	let
lose	lost	lost
make	made	made
mean	meant	meant
meet	met	met
pay	paid	paid
put	put	put
read	read	read
ring	rang	rung
run	ran	run
say	said	said
see	saw	seen
sell	sold	sold
send	sent	sent
speak	spoke	spoken
take	took	taken
tell	told	told
think	thought	thought
understand	understood	understood
wear	wore	worn
withdraw	withdrew	withdrawn
write	wrote	written

Irregular comparative and superlative forms of adjectives

Adjective	Comparative	Superlative
bad	worse	worst
far	farther	farthest
good	better	best
little	less	least
many/a lot of	more	most
much/a lot of	more	most

Verbs followed by gerunds

appreciate	enjoy	postpone
avoid	explain	practice
can't help	feel like	prevent
consider	finish	quit
delay	imagine	recommend
detest	keep	risk
discuss	mind	suggest
dislike	miss	understand

Verbs followed by infinitives

afford	decide	offer
agree	expect	plan
appear	help	prepare
ask	hope	promise
arrange	hurry	request
be sure	intend	seem
can't afford	learn	want
can't wait	manage	wish
choose	need	would like

Verbs followed by gerunds or infinitives

begin	hate	remember
can't stand	like	start
continue	love	try
forget	prefer	

Verbs followed by objects and infinitives

advise	force	promise *
allow	help *	remind
ask *	hire	require
cause	invite	teach
choose *	need *	tell
convince	order	want *
encourage	pay *	warn
expect *	permit	would like *

* Words with a star can also be followed by an infinitive without an object.

How to spell the gerund and the present participle

Add -<u>ing</u> to the base form of the verb.

        speak   speaking

If the base form ends in -<u>e</u>, drop the -<u>e</u> and add -<u>ing</u>.

        have   having

In verbs of one syllable, if the last three letters are a consonant-vowel-consonant (C-V-C) series, double the last consonant and then add -<u>ing</u>.

        C V C
        ↓ ↓ ↓
        s i t   sitting

Exception: Don't double the last consonant in words that end in -<u>w</u>, -<u>x</u>, or -<u>y</u>.

        fix   fixing

In verbs of more than one syllable that end in a consonant-vowel-consonant series, double the last consonant <u>only</u> if the stress is on the last syllable.

        permít   permitting
but not   órder   ordering

ABC

COMPANY

AN EQUAL OPPORTUNITY EMPLOYER

Please complete all requested information. Use ink and print.

GENERAL INFORMATION

TODAY'S DATE	DATE AVAILABLE FOR WORK:

NAME: LAST   FIRST   MIDDLE

SOCIAL SECURITY NUMBER

STREET ADDRESS

CITY   STATE   ZIP

TELEPHONE (HOME):   TELEPHONE (WORK):

IF YOU HAVE WORKED FOR OUR COMPANY BEFORE, STATE WHERE, WHEN, FINAL POSITION AND REASON FOR LEAVING:

HAVE YOU EVER APPLIED TO OUR COMPANY BEFORE? _____ YES _____ NO

IF YES, WHERE:

HAVE YOU EVER BEEN CONVICTED OF A CRIME BY A CIVILIAN OR MILITARY COURT: _____ YES _____ NO

POSITION DESIRED:	SALARY DESIRED:

FULL TIME _____ 35+ HRS PER WK   PART TIME _____ LESS THAN 35 HRS

AGE (IF YOU ARE UNDER 18 YOU MAY HAVE TO PROVIDE A WORK PERMIT BEFORE STARTING WORK)

ARE YOU AT LEAST 18 YRS OLD? _____ YES _____ NO

ARE YOU AT LEAST 16 YRS OLD? _____ YES _____ NO

PLEASE INDICATE THE HOURS (BOTH DAY AND EVENING YOU ARE AVAILABLE TO WORK:

SUN _____ MON _____ TUES _____ WED _____

THURS _____ FRI _____ SAT _____

NOTE: ALTHOUGH EVERY EFFORT TO ACCOMMODATE INDIVIDUAL PREFERENCES WILL BE MADE, BUSINESS NEEDS MAY REQUIRE ANY OR ALL OF THE FOLLOWING: EXTENSION OF HOURS, A ROTATING WORK SCHEDULE, SATURDAY AND/OR SUNDAY HOURS, OVERTIME

DO YOU HAVE ANY RELATIVES EMPLOYED BY OUR COMPANY? _____ YES _____ NO

IF YES, IDENTIFY BY NAME AND LOCATION

WORK EXPERIENCE (START WITH CURRENT EMPLOYER AND CONTINUE WITH FORMER EMPLOYERS

EMPLOYER #1

ADDRESS	CITY	STATE	ZIP
PHONE	SUPERVISOR	TITLE	
POSITION	FINAL SALARY	REASON FOR LEAVING	

DATES ON EMPLOYMENT:
FROM: TO:

EMPLOYER #2

ADDRESS	CITY	STATE	ZIP
PHONE	SUPERVISOR	TITLE	
POSITION	FINAL SALARY	REASON FOR LEAVING	

DATES ON EMPLOYMENT:
FROM: TO:

EMPLOYER #3

ADDRESS	CITY	STATE	ZIP
PHONE	SUPERVISOR	TITLE	
POSITION	FINAL SALARY	REASON FOR LEAVING	

DATES ON EMPLOYMENT:
FROM: TO:

EMPLOYER #4

ADDRESS	CITY	STATE	ZIP
PHONE	SUPERVISOR	TITLE	
POSITION	FINAL SALARY	REASON FOR LEAVING	

DATES ON EMPLOYMENT:
FROM: TO:

PROFESSIONAL REFERENCES - LIST PERSONS FAMILIAR WITH YOUR WORK ABILITY (EXCLUDE RELATIVES)

NAME	PHONE NUMBER	HOW ACQUAINTED	HOW LONG
NAME	PHONE NUMBER	HOW ACQUAINTED	HOW LONG
NAME	PHONE NUMBER	HOW ACQUAINTED	HOW LONG

EMERGENCY CONTACT

IN CASE OF EMERGENCY, CONTACT (NAME):	(PHONE NUMBER):

- -

DO NOT WRITE BELOW THIS LINE.

(HIRING PERSONNEL: COMPLETE THIS SECTION ONLY AFTER AN OFFER OF EMPLOYMENT IS MADE.)

JOB TITLE	T (TEMP OR R (REG)	FT OR PT	STORE #	MALE OR FEMALE	START DATE
DATE OF BIRTH	HOURLY OR COEFF. MGR. OR SALARIED (PAY TYPE: CIRCLE ONE)	RATE: (ONLY IF HOURLY): _____ PER HOUR		NEXT REVIEW DATE	
RACE (CIRCLE ONE) WHITE - BLACK - HISPANIC - ASIAN/PACIFIC ISLAND - AMERICAN INDIAN		SIGNATURE OF HIRING INDIVIDUAL:		YES OR NO REQUEST BACKGROUND: CIRCLE ONE	

(Continued on page 152.)

(Continued from page 151.)

EDUCATION AND TRAINING

SCHOOL	PLEASE PRINT NAME, STREET, CITY, & ZIP FOR EACH SCHOOL	NUMBER OF YEARS COMPLETED	TYPE OF COURSE/MAJOR
COLLEGE			
HIGH SCHOOL			
ADDITIONAL TRAINING			

INDICATE THE JOB SKILLS WHICH YOU HAVE PERFORMED:
_____ TYPING (_____) WPM _____ COMPUTER SOFTWARE (LIST: _____) _____ OTHER

ADDITIONAL INQUIRES

HAVE YOU EVER BEEN DISMISSED OR ASKED TO RESIGN FROM ANY EMPLOYER? _____ YES _____ NO

IF YES, PLEASE EXPLAIN: _____

IF EMPLOYMENT IS OFFERED, CAN YOU PROVIDE VERIFICATION OF YOUR LEGAL RIGHT TO WORK IN THE U.S.? _____ YES _____ NO

WHY ARE YOU INTERESTED IN WORKING FOR OUR COMPANY? _____

WHAT DIDN'T YOU LIKE ABOUT YOUR PREVIOUS JOBS? _____

PROVIDE INFORMATION ABOUT COMMUNITY ACTIVITIES, PROFESSIONAL TRADE OR SERVICE ORGANIZATIONS TO WHICH YOU BELONG WHICH YOU BELIEVE MAY DEMONSTRATE YOUR JOB RELATED ABILITIES (YOU MAY EXCLUDE THOSE WHICH INDICATE RACE, COLOR, RELIGION, SEX, NATIONAL ORIGIN, AGE, HANDICAP.)

REFERRAL SOURCE

_____ WALK-IN APPLICANT	_____ AGENCY	_____ EMPLOYEE REFERRAL	_____ NEWSPAPER	_____ OTHER
	NAME OF AGENCY:	NAME OF EMPLOYEE:		PLEASE LIST:

IF HIRED, I AGREE TO ABIDE BY THE RULES AND REGULATIONS OF THE COMPANY. I UNDERSTAND THAT MY EMPLOYMENT IS AT-WILL. THIS MEANS THAT I DO NOT HAVE A CONTRACT OF EMPLOYMENT FOR ANY PARTICULAR DURATION OR LIMITING THE GROUNDS FOR MY TERMINATION IN ANY WAY. I AM FREE TO RESIGN AT ANY TIME. SIMILARLY, THE COMPANY IS FREE TO TERMINATE OR CHANGE THE TERMS AND/OR CONDITIONS OF MY EMPLOYMENT AT ANY TIME FOR ANY REASON OR NO REASON. THE ONLY TIME MY AT-WILL STATUS COULD BE CHANGED IS IF I WERE TO ENTER INTO A WRITTEN CONTRACT WITH THE COMPANY EXPLICITLY PROMISING ME JOB SECURITY.

ALL OF THE INFORMATION I HAVE SUPPLIED IN THIS APPLICATION IS A TRUE AND COMPLETE STATEMENT OF THE FACTS, AN IF EMPLOYED, ANY OMISSIONS OR FALSE OF MISLEADING STATEMENTS ON THIS APPLICATION OR DURING THE INTERVIEW PROCESS COULD RESULT IN IMMEDIATE DISMISSAL REGARDLESS OF WHEN SUCH INFORMATION IS DISCOVERED. I FURTHER AUTHORIZE ALL COURTS, PROBATION DEPARTMENTS, PROSECUTOR'S OFFICES, BOARDS, EMPLOYERS, EDUCATIONAL AND CREDIT COMPANIES, OTHER INSTITUTIONS AND AGENCIES, WITHOUT EXCEPTION, TO FURNISH THE COMPANY OR ITS REPRESENTATIVES ANY INFORMATION ANY OF THEM HAVE CONCERNING ME. THIS WAIVER DOES NOT PERMIT THE RELEASE OR USE OF DISABILITY-RELATED OR MEDICAL INFORMATION IN A MANNER PROHIBITED BY THE AMERICANS WITH DISABILITIES ACT (ADA) AND OTHER RELEVANT FEDERAL AND STATE LAWS. I FURTHER AUTHORIZE A CHECK BY ANY CONSUMER AGENCY OF MY EMPLOYMENT HISTORY AS WELL AS ANY INCIDENTS OF EMPLOYMENT DISHONESTY, RETAIL THEFT OR CRIMINAL ACTIVITY. I UNDERSTAND THAT MY EMPLOYMENT AND/OR RETENTION MAY BE AFFECTED IN WHOLE OR IN PART BY A REPORT RECEIVED FROM THIS AGENCY. I HEREBY DISCHARGE AND EXONERATE THE COMPANY, ITS AGENTS AND REPRESENTATIVES, OR ANY PERSON SO FURNISHING INFORMATION, FROM ANY LIABILITY AND ALL LIABILITY OF EVERY NATURE AND KIND ARISING OUT OF THE FURNISHING, INSPECTION OR COLLECTION OF SUCH DOCUMENTS, RECORDS, AND OTHER INFORMATION OR THE INVESTIGATION MADE BY THE COMPANY. A PHOTOSTATIC COPY OF THIS AUTHORIZATION WILL BE CONSIDERED AS EFFECTIVE AND VALID AS THE ORIGINAL (WHEREVER LEGALLY REQUIRED, A COPY OF ANY CREDIT REPORT AN OTHER INFORMATION WILL BE AVAILABLE UPON MY REQUEST.)

I AGREE TO PROTECT THE COMPANY'S CONFIDENTIAL INFORMATION, TRADE SECRETS, AND OTHER PROPRIETARY INFORMATION AND WILL NOT REVEAL SUCH INFORMATION TO ANYONE AT ANY TIME DURING OR AFTER CESSATION OF MY EMPLOYMENT.

I FURTHER UNDERSTAND THAT THE COMPANY WILL NOT EMPLOY PERSONS WHO USE ILLEGAL DRUGS OR ENGAGE IN SUBSTANCE ABUSE, AND THAT THE COMPANY RETAINS THE RIGHT TO SCREEN FROM EMPLOYMENT SUCH INDIVIDUALS.

IF HIRED, I UNDERSTAND THAT THE FIRST 90 DAYS OF EMPLOYMENT ARE CONSIDERED A PROBATIONARY PERIOD, DURING WHICH TIME I WILL NOT BE CONSIDERED A REGULAR EMPLOYEE. I WILL BE CONSIDERED A REGULAR EMPLOYEE AFTER I HAVE SUCCESSFULLY COMPLETED THIS PROBATIONARY PERIOD.

_____   _____
SIGNATURE OF APPLICANT   DATE

(THIS APPLICATION WILL ONLY BE CONSIDERED FOR 3 MONTHS. AFTER THAT TIME, YOU MUST COMPLETE A NEW APPLICATION FOR FURTHER CONSIDERATION.)

CITYMALL FLOOR PLAN

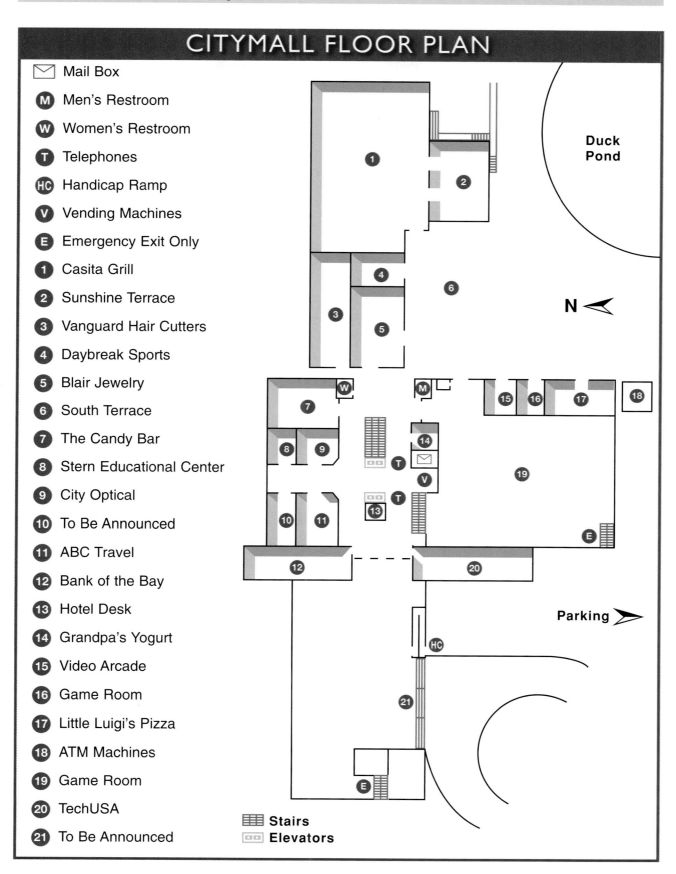

✉ Mail Box
Ⓜ Men's Restroom
Ⓦ Women's Restroom
Ⓣ Telephones
ⒽⒸ Handicap Ramp
Ⓥ Vending Machines
Ⓔ Emergency Exit Only
❶ Casita Grill
❷ Sunshine Terrace
❸ Vanguard Hair Cutters
❹ Daybreak Sports
❺ Blair Jewelry
❻ South Terrace
❼ The Candy Bar
❽ Stern Educational Center
❾ City Optical
❿ To Be Announced
⓫ ABC Travel
⓬ Bank of the Bay
⓭ Hotel Desk
⓮ Grandpa's Yogurt
⓯ Video Arcade
⓰ Game Room
⓱ Little Luigi's Pizza
⓲ ATM Machines
⓳ Game Room
⓴ TechUSA
㉑ To Be Announced

Duck Pond

N

Parking

▦ Stairs
▣ Elevators

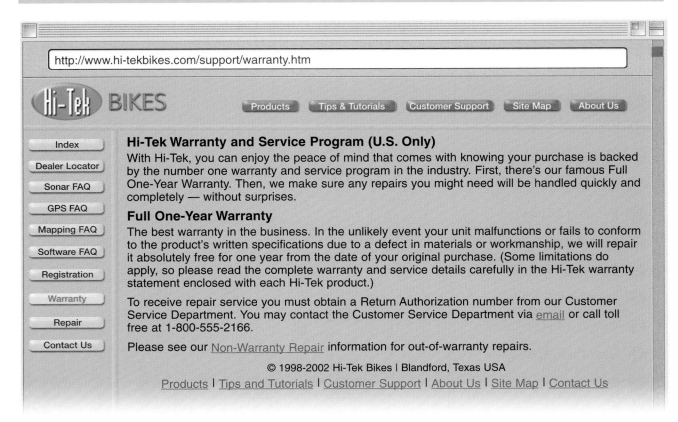

http://www.hi-tekbikes.com/support/warranty.htm

Hi-Tek BIKES

Products | Tips & Tutorials | Customer Support | Site Map | About Us

Index
Dealer Locator
Sonar FAQ
GPS FAQ
Mapping FAQ
Software FAQ
Registration
Warranty
Repair
Contact Us

Hi-Tek Warranty and Service Program (U.S. Only)

With Hi-Tek, you can enjoy the peace of mind that comes with knowing your purchase is backed by the number one warranty and service program in the industry. First, there's our famous Full One-Year Warranty. Then, we make sure any repairs you might need will be handled quickly and completely — without surprises.

Full One-Year Warranty

The best warranty in the business. In the unlikely event your unit malfunctions or fails to conform to the product's written specifications due to a defect in materials or workmanship, we will repair it absolutely free for one year from the date of your original purchase. (Some limitations do apply, so please read the complete warranty and service details carefully in the Hi-Tek warranty statement enclosed with each Hi-Tek product.)

To receive repair service you must obtain a Return Authorization number from our Customer Service Department. You may contact the Customer Service Department via email or call toll free at 1-800-555-2166.

Please see our Non-Warranty Repair information for out-of-warranty repairs.

© 1998-2002 Hi-Tek Bikes | Blandford, Texas USA

Products | Tips and Tutorials | Customer Support | About Us | Site Map | Contact Us

---

BLACK
B 246-D

PRODUCT DESCRIPTION:
PICTON F3 CAMERA

Retain this Worldwide Warranty with proof of purchase for your records.

PICTON

ONE YEAR WORLDWIDE LIMITED WARRANTY

(Excluding the Continental United States, Alaska, Hawaii, Puerto Rico, and the U.S. Virgin Islands.)

Welcome to the worldwide family of Picton users:

Your Picton equipment has been manufactured to the highest quality standards by PICTON, INC. Newark, NJ, USA.

This Picton product, except for batteries, is warranted by PICTON, INC. to be free from defects in materials or workmanship for a period of one year from the date of purchase. During this period any one of Picton's worldwide repair facilities will repair without charge any parts or assembly of parts found to be defective in material or workmanship subject to the following limitations:

1. This warranty extends to the original consumer purchaser only and is not assignable or transferable.
2. This warranty shall not extend to any product which has been subject to misuse, abuse, negligence, accident or unauthorized repair.

All warranties implied by law including any warranty of merchantability shall be of a duration of one (1) year from date of purchase. The warranties herein are expressly in lieu of all other express warranties including the payment of consequential or incidental damages for the breach of any warranty.

No warranties, whether express or implied, including the warranties of merchantability or fitness for a particular purpose are made by any distributor or dealer, of the product herein warranted; nor shall such dealer or distributor be liable for the payment of any direct incidental or consequential damages.

In order to obtain worldwide service, the consumer should return the Picton product, either in person or addressed to the Warranty Department or any Picton authorized service repair station, together with proof of purchase and this warranty. The original consumer in returning this product must prepay all postage, shipping, transportation, insurance and delivery costs to the repair facility.

LAST NAME

FIRST NAME

ADDRESS

CITY   **STATE**

ZIP

JetBus Bus Company
Post Office Box 36201
San Antonio, Texas 78205
210-555-1450

www.jetfast.com

> >

July 2, 2003

Ms. Clarita Guzman
202 East Pine Street, #8A
Kingston, IL 60026

Dear Ms. Guzman:

I was very sorry to learn about your disappointing experience with JetBus and apologize for our delay in responding.

We know that your time is valuable and realize that this must have been frustrating. I regret the inconvenience and can promise you that we are working very hard to prevent schedule irregularities and to improve our overall on-time performance.

We want to encourage you to ride with us again soon and hope that you will have the opportunity to use the enclosed toward the purchase of future JetBus travel.

Please accept our apology and give us the opportunity to regain your confidence.

Sincerely,

Mike McKenna

Michael McKenna
Manager
Consumer Affairs

MTM:mrx

Enclosure

> >

Employment Standards Administration Wage and Hour Division

. . . .

General Information on The Fair Labor Standards Act

Child Labor: An employee must be at least **16** years old to work in most non-farm jobs and at least **18** to work in non-farm jobs declared hazardous by the Secretary of Labor. Youths **14** and **15** years old may work outside school hours in various non-manufacturing, non-mining, non-hazardous jobs under the following conditions:

No more than –

   3 hours on a school day or **18** hours in a school week;

   8 hours on a non-school day or **40** hours in a non-school week.

Also, work may not begin before 7 a.m. or end after 7 p.m., except from June 1 through Labor Day, when evening hours are extended to 9 p.m. Different rules apply in agricultural employment.

ENFORCEMENT: The Department of Labor may recover back wages, either administratively or through court action, for the employees that have been underpaid in violation of the law. Violations may result in civil or criminal action.

Fines of up to $10,000 per violation may be assessed against employers who violate the child labor provisions of the law and up to $1,000 per violation against employers who willfully or repeatedly violate the minimum wage or overtime pay provisions. The law prohibits discriminating against or discharging workers who file a complaint or participate in any proceedings under the Act.

Note:
• Certain occupations and establishments are exempt from the minimum wage and/or overtime pay provisions.
• Special provisions apply to workers in American Samoa.
• Where state law requires a higher minimum wage, the higher standard applies.

FOR ADDITIONAL INFORMATION, contact the nearest Wage and Hour Division office — listed in most telephone directories under United States Government, Labor Department.

. . . .

⑤ Five-Star Uniforms

P.O. Box 306, San Miguel, NM 87503
Phone:(505) 555-9860 Fax: (505) 555-9861

Date: _____

Firm: _____

ATTN: _____

Address: _____

City, State, Zip: _____

Phone: _____ Fax: _____

Qty.	Item #	Color	Size	Description	Unit Price	Total

Item #	Color	Price Sizes 36–46 Short, Reg & Tall	Price Sizes 48 Short, Reg & Tall; 50 Reg & Tall	Price Sizes 52 Reg & Tall; 54–56 Reg
3399NV	Navy Coveralls	$23.50	$30.00	$33.50
3399KH	Khaki Coveralls	$23.50	$30.00	$33.50
3399GY	Gray Coveralls	$23.50	$30.00	Not Available
3399MB	Medium Blue Coveralls	$23.50	$30.00	Not Available
3399RD	Crimson Red Coveralls	$23.50	$30.00 (no 48 short)	Not Available

Turnaround delivery time 10–14 business days.
Only UPS Ground freight available.

With your help, it's all falling into place.

FOR YOUR HEALTH

Patient: MAYER, PETER   Dr. JOHNSON, LEON

Medication: MOBIC 7.5 MG TABLET B-I   Pharmacy Phone: (973) 555-1234

Directions: TAKE 1 TABLET DAILY   Rx NO.   382-812X

WHY AM I TAKING THIS DRUG?

For arthritic conditions, pain, inflammation, fever.

HOW DO I STORE THIS?

Store at room temperature away from moisture and sunlight. Do not store in the bathroom.

HOW SHOULD I TAKE IT?

Take with food/antacid as directed. Tell MD of other drugs you use/diseases you have, allergies or if pregnant. Limit alcohol intake.

IF I SHOULD MISS A DOSE?

Take missed dose as soon as remembered but not if it is almost time for the the next dose. Do not "double-up" the doses.

ARE THERE ANY SIDE EFFECTS?

Dizziness, drowsiness. Report eye/ear problems, urine color change, black stools, difficulty breathing, mental changes, sun sensitivity, stomach pain.

Refill Your Prescription On-Line at WWW.FORYOURHEALTH.COM

This information is an educational service and does not address all possible uses, actions, precautions, interactions, or side effects of this medicine. If you desire any additional prescriptions counseling, please ask your pharmacist or your doctor.

Over-the-Counter Medications are Drugs, Too

Literally thousands of drugs are available for purchase "over-the-counter" (OTC), which means that a person does not need a prescription to purchase them. Just because these drugs can be purchased without a doctor's prescription does not mean they are harmless. Many of these drugs have side effects, which must be listed on the package. Especially for older adults who also may be on prescription medications, taking OTCs may alter the effect of the prescribed medicine. Always check with a pharmacist or physician about possible drug interactions before adding any medication.

A directory of common OTC ingredients, categorized by ailment, is listed below. Only the actual, active ingredients are given. Compare these ingredients with the ingredients listed on the outside of the packages.

Allergies, Coughs, and Colds

Most OTCs for colds or allergies contain a "shotgun" of ingredients aimed at multiple symptoms. Often, a person can take only one ingredient instead of the combinations offered and can then avoid the side effects from the medications they do not need. It does not make sense to take more medication than necessary to relieve symptoms. Remember, these medications will not cure a cold — they only relieve symptoms.

Decongestants: Phenylephrine, ephedrine, phenylpropanolamine (PPA), or other words ending with "-ephrine" or "-edrine."

Antihistamine: Chlorpheniramine or pyrilamine, or often words ending with "-amine."

Expectorants: Glyceryl guaiacolate and potassium iodide. The effectiveness of expectorants is unproved.

Cough suppressant: Dextromethorphan hydrobromide.

Constipation

More than 700 OTC laxative products are available to the American public, making us a "super bowel-conscious" society. Only the most popular types are listed below. As one noted authority pointed out, "It's sometimes better to flush laxatives directly down the toilet without first passing them through the human body."

Bisacodyl, phenolphthalein, castor oil: Stimulant/irritant type of laxatives (the ones which are least desirable).

Epsom salt (magnesium sulfate), magnesium hydroxide, magnesium citrate: Saline cathartics, which remain in the intestines.

Mineral oil, dioctyl sodium sulfosuccinate, dioctyl calcium sulfo-succinate: Fecal softeners which make elimination easier.

Psyllium seed, methylcellulose, sodium carboxymethyl-cellulose, and tragacanth: Bulk forming laxatives, which form a soft bolus of material which promotes bowel movement.

Upset Stomach

Effervescent antacids: Contain sodium bicarbonate (baking soda), potassium bicarbonate, and citric acid. Should be used sparingly and occasionally.

Aluminum hydroxide: An effective antacid that will not cause stomach acid rebound.

Magnesium hydroxide: Often combined with aluminum hydroxide, because this product is a known laxative and antacid.

Simethicone: Also called polydimethylsiloxane. The FDA has ruled this product to be ineffective in relieving gas.

Pain, Fever, and Headache

Aspirin: Probably one of the most important OTC drugs. Americans consume almost 19 billion aspirin tablets per year. Aspirin is effective in reducing fever, pain, and inflammation. Aspirin, however, is associated with increased stomach irritation, bleeding time, and "ringing in the ears."

Acetaminophen: Usually no side effects. Does not cause gastrointestinal bleeding sometimes associated with aspirin. However, taken in large doses or for extended periods, it can cause liver damage.

Ibuprofen: Although touted to be easier on the stomach than aspirin, the prescription formula of this product advises that it be taken with food.

Diarrhea

Although many OTC ingredients are purported to alleviate the symptoms of diarrhea, the FDA has stated that none effectively relieve diarrhea symptoms. Alumina powder, attapulgite, belladonna alkaloids, bismuth salts, calcium carbonate, calcium hydroxide, sodium carboxymethylcellulose, charcoal, kaolin, pectin, salol, and zinc phenolsulfonate are among the most commonly used ingredients in antidiarrheal medication. Most bouts of diarrhea will spontaneously clear. Consult physician if high fever accompanies the diarrhea or if the diarrhea lasts for more than two days.

Apply today for the
Adventure Diamond Card

Adventure Diamond offers you these superior benefits:

- *0% introductory APR° on purchases*
- *No annual fee*
- *Up to 2% Moneyback Bonus*
- *Internet Account access and bill payment*
- *Superior 24-hour customer service*
- *$500,000 travel accidental death insurance†*
- *$25,000 auto rental coverage†*
- *Plus many more privileges*

No other card rewards you like the no-annual-fee Adventure Diamond Card. You'll enjoy an unbeatable 0% introductory APR° on purchases! So apply for your Card right away and enjoy no interest on purchases for the next 5 billing periods†.

Plus, you'll receive up to a 2% Moneyback Bonus award°. You will earn a Moneyback Bonus award of up to 1%, paid yearly, based on your annual level and type of purchases. Then exchange your award check for certificates worth double your award amount from select partners (see back).

You'll also enjoy great discounts at our Internet site, superior 24-hour Cardmember service and much more. So apply for your Adventure Diamond today. It's the only Card you'll need!

APPLY TODAY!

†See Important Information Section.
°Certain restrictions apply. See reverse side for details.

There's always something more to
Adventure
Diamond

▲ Detach here ▼

Adventure Diamond Card Application

IMPORTANT: PLEASE PRINT USING CAPITAL LETTERS AND COMPLETE ALL INFORMATION.

Step 1   Please tell us about yourself

| FIRST | MIDDLE | LAST NAME | | DATE OF BIRTH (MO., DAY, YR.) M M D D Y Y |

HOME ADDRESS | APT. NO | CITY | STATE | ZIP CODE

HOME TELEPHONE* ( ) | WORK TELEPHONE ( ) | SOCIAL SECURITY NUMBER*

DO YOU □ OWN □ RENT □ OTHER | HOUSING PAYMENT* (per month) $ | LENGTH OF TIME AT PRESENT ADDRESS YEARS Y Y | MONTHS M M

ARE YOU A U.S. CITIZEN OR PERMANENT U.S. RESIDENT? □ YES □ NO | MOTHER'S MAIDEN NAME (for security purposes)

Step 2   Please tell us about your household finances

EMPLOYER

OCCUPATION | HOW LONG?

EMPLOYER'S CITY/STATE/ZIP

DO YOU HAVE A □ SAVINGS ACCOUNT □ CHECKING ACCOUNT

YOUR ANNUAL SALARY $ _____
PLUS BONUS + $ _____
OTHER HOUSEHOLD INCOME†
TOTAL HOUSEHOLD INCOME† $ _ , _ _ _ , _ _ _

* This information is required to complete this application.

† Alimony, child support, spouse's income or separate maintenance income need not be disclosed if you do not wish to have it considered as a basis for paying this obligation. Minimum Annual Household Income of $15,000 required for any Adventure Card Account. If you are relying on the income of another person to qualify for an Account and would like to apply with co-applicant, see Important Information section. For highest credit line, please include all sources of Annual Household income.

Free additional Card (Complete below)
Yes, please send me an additional Card at no extra cost for:

PRINT NAME OF AUTHORIZED USER (FIRST, MIDDLE INITIAL, LAST NAME)

Step 3   Please sign below

I understand that my credit line will be set after you have reviewed my financial information. I have read and agree to the Important Information on the back. I certify that I am 18 years of age or older and that the information provided is accurate.

X _____ / _____
SIGNATURE   DATE

Send in your application online at Adventurecard.com today.

Pasadena Classified
Line Advertising Coupon

Yes!

Run My Pre-Paid Line Classified Ad
In The Next Issue $10.00 For 20 Words
20¢ For Each Additional Word

Office Use Only

Operator	# Weeks

Category _____

Name _____

Address _____

Telephone _____

Cost per week _____

Number of weeks _____

Total amount _____

My payment of $_____ enclosed

Please charge my Visa/MC

Card # _____

Expiration date _____

Mail to: Pasadena Classifieds, P.O. Box 950, Monrovia, CA 91016 • Classified Deadline Tuesday 11:00 am